ANTHOLOGY OF LOVE AND DEATH
VOL. 1

ANTHOLOGY OF LOVE AND DEATH VOL. 1

MARIE JOSEPH-CHARLES

Madison Schleibaum

Contents

Dedication   ix

1	Love Spell	1
2	This Road	32
3	Disobedience	34
4	The Witness	44
5	What Needed to be Done	59
6	To be a queen	90
7	Tea	91
8	The Resurrection of Magic	115
9	My Knight	129
10	The Most Terrifying Question	132
11	I don't know; I'm just typing	135
12	A Breakup	137
13	Muerte, New Mexico	142
14	Twinkle Sparkle	168

15	Forgive Yourself	170
16	End of Days	172
17	Nothing Rhymes with Orange	174
18	Brick by Brick	176
19	Fortune Teller	177
20	Side by Side	179
21	Condemn my Soul	183
22	Free write Aug 20, 2023	184
23	Stand and Fall	185
24	Sabine	187
25	H.	200
26	Today	202
27	The Heating	204
28	My Own Story	207
29	Written in the Hotel in Chicago	215
30	Love and Lust	217
31	Flower Mirror	219
32	Turkey Shoot	221
33	Shadow, shadow.	230
34	An Excerpt from Angel's Seed	232
35	If I Died Tomorrow	234

| 36 | The Ornament | 236 |
| 37 | New Year | 245 |

Copyright © 2024 by Madison Schleibaum

All rights reserved. No part of this book may be reproduced in any manner whatsoever without written permission except in the case of brief quotations embodied in critical articles and reviews.

First Printing, 2024

In dedication to the wonderful people who have supported my novels, poetry, and short stories.

I

Love Spell

I watched the flame go out and I knew it was all over.

But let me start at the beginning. My Auntie Dorinda, my great aunt, was known as a little... eccentric in the neighborhood but people would come to her shop from all over the United States. Her shop was called The Verdant Apothecary. As a young botanist, she had traveled the world learning about the healing properties of various flowers, herbs, and roots. She studied with traditional healers, town elders, witch doctors, and other scholars. She then brought that information back home to our little corner of Illinois and set up to share her knowledge out of a little storefront in the suburbs of Chicago.

Many of her teas were grown on the two-acre plot we lived on far outside of the city. She grew lavender, chamomile, three different varieties of roses, chrysanthemums, dandelions, conifers, and milk thistle. For the rest, she had suppliers from all of the various continents she had made friends on over the years. She had standard teas that helped with things like sleeping and constipation but she also had jars upon jars of flowers, roots, and herbs that she would mix to create personalized concoctions.

The basement below the shop, however, was where the real magic happened. Every once in a while, someone would come along and ask to speak to Aunt Dori in private. She would escort them down the stairs and ask Cassandra to watch over the shop.

Cassandra was maybe two or so years older than me and a stray that Aunt Dori had picked up in a village in Bolivia. She was an orphan around five years old who was picking out of a trash can. She was chased away by an older boy with a stick and ran right into Dori's leg. Without hesitation, my aunt scooped up the scared little girl and took her back to the house of the family she was staying with. They informed her that the girl's parents had died and there had been no one to take her in so she'd been living on the street for almost a year. The next day, Dori packed up her research and clothes and headed to La Paz with the little girl in tow. After a great legal battle, the rest, as they say, is history. Cassandra became my Aunt's right hand and the closest thing she had to a daughter. She traveled the world with her, learning the powers of the herbs and medicines, and eventually ran the business side of the shop.

For as long as I could remember, Cassie had been fun and outgoing but always had her nose in a book and her hair in a tight bun on top of her head, giving her the look of an underage librarian. I don't think she ever actually watched an episode of ANYTHING on television until they stopped traveling. She was impressively smart and could speak five languages fluently and three conversationally by the time she was a teenager. I truthfully found her intimidating but still loved to spend time with her when they were in the country for the holidays.

I came into Dori and Cassie's lives permanently when my mom and dad were killed in a car accident. I was ten years old at the time. Dori, being Dori, hardly batted an eye at the thought of being my guardian. Unlike Cassie, however, I didn't get to travel the world. I was put in boarding school not because Aunt Dori didn't want me, but because she had promised her niece, my mother, as she lay dying in the hospital, that she would give me every advantage she could in life. She thought boarding school would be the way to do that. In her mind, allowing me to hobnob with rich, snooty girls would help me make the right connections to become successful instead of traveling the world and living in tents on the outskirts of civilization like a vagrant. When I was fifteen and getting ready to start high school, I broke down sobbing and told her how I felt about boarding school. I felt disconnected from everyone and everything I knew. I hadn't grown up in country clubs and with a nanny like the other girls and couldn't relate to them at all. They bullied me for being what they considered poor. I hated the dormitories and pressure. Aunt Dori tried to comfort me and Cassie, having no idea how I felt, patted my back. Auntie made me some tea to soothe my nerves and I honestly have no recollection of the rest of the night.

The following morning at the breakfast table, Auntie

Dorinda announced the creation of The Verdant Apothecary and that I would be attending the public high school fifteen minutes away. I was overjoyed at the thought of a normal life in a normal high school but then a dark cloud moved into me.

"But, Aunt Dori, what about your traveling and your research?" I had asked.

"What do you think all this research has been for? It's been to share it with the world. I think your education is just the motivation I need to make that happen. Besides, I'm getting too old for these long flights. They flair up my sciatica."

I knew that was a lie. Aunt Dori wasn't even sixty years old yet at the time.

"Promise I'm not holding you back?"

She smiled a gentle, warm smile and touched my hair. "Never."

She leased a small, 900sqft space with a basement next door to a bank. She filled the dark wooden shelves that went from the floor to ceiling with glass jars of flowers, dried leaves, dried roots, and tinctures. She kept the most valuable ones in a locked case behind the front desk. She had little silk bags to make your own teabags and bottles to mix her own brews just for you. Dried sticks and flowers hung from ribbons from the ceiling and over the doors. She was a witch who performed magic with seemingly simple things. She somehow managed to find time to publish her book – also called *The Verdant Apothecary* – which made quite a bit of money.

That fall I attended a normal high school and had normal friends. Cassie, having a childhood wildly different from mine, chose to continue homeschooling. She studied at the apothecary and after school every day I would ride the bus from the suburbs and take the L out of the city and walk four blocks to the shop. Cassie and I would do our homework at the front counter but I found myself listening to my aunt talk to clients and explain the different properties of the contents of her jars. I found myself more interested in her than my books and took to reading hers when I had the time.

Dori realized I was taking notes and couldn't have been more thrilled. She began tutoring me while Cassie, who had passed her GED a year early, was at the community college for business management. Everything seemed so simple. I thought I knew our inventory as well as Cassie did. I didn't even know Aunt Dori had anything more than backstock in the basement until I saw her come out of it with a woman who was crying and holding a box and thanking my great aunt profusely.

"What's that all about?" I asked her.

"She just needed something a little stronger," Aunt Dori smiled and turned to tend to another customer.

"What's down there?"

Her smile left almost instantly as she turned back toward me. "When you are ready, I will tell you. But you must never go down there until I say. Understand?"

I didn't understand why she was being so secretive but I understood that she was serious and so I nodded.

After high school, I continued to work at the shop. Cassie specialized in handling the vendors. Her skills as a polyglot were exceptionally useful and her degree in business management made me slightly envious. I wanted to be useful for more than just stocking shelves and chatting with the regulars. In the spring and summer, I would tend the plants we grew, making sure they were pest-free and drying them properly. But it just didn't feel like enough.

I was twenty years old and it was a hot, summer day. Cassie was fussing over her laptop and yelling into the phone in Cantonese. A woman entered the shop. She was sobbing and holding a candle. Cassie's eyes nearly popped out of her head. She said something hastily into the phone and dropped it while fleeing for the basement. Auntie Dorinda emerged and took her into an embrace before leading the woman with the candle down the stairs.

I looked at the now-closed basement door and over to Cassie. She was standing with both her hands covering her mouth and shaking her head.

"What was that about?" I asked her. Cassie just shook her head harder. "Cass!"

She snapped out of her trance and looked at me. "The candle went out," she whispered.

"And? It can't be relit?"

Cassie shook her head. "You can't bring back the dead."

"Bring back the dead? What are you talking about?"

Cassie looked at me with a troubled expression. She seemed to be debating the divulgence of some vital piece of information.

"Cass. What's going on?" I looked her in the eye.

She looked back at the basement door before leading me by the elbow to the other end of the empty store behind a shelf of Chinese herbs. She breathed heavily, still wrestling with something internally.

"Cassandra? What is it?" I put my hand on her shoulder.

She bit her lip. "Do you think we can afford our life just

selling tea and books?" I stared at her blankly. "Do you know what is in the basement?" I shook my head. She inhaled. "I should not be telling you this. I should not."

"Someone just came in with a candle and you freaked out. Yes, you should tell me. I am as much a part of this shop as you are," I felt defiant, knowing Aunt Dori would not want Cassie to be the one to tell me.

She chewed her lip some more. "Dorinda is a very skilled witch. In the basement is where she performs dark magic. The magic she doesn't want you exposed to. Some of the online orders I ship out aren't online orders at all. They are dangerous potions going to wealthy clients."

I stifled a laugh. "Auntie Dori? An actual witch?" Cassie stared at me without even a hint of humor. "You're serious?" She nodded. "Then what's with the candle?"

"That was a love spell. It makes you the object of your chosen one's desire. You have until the wick is spent to make them fall in love with you in earnest."

"But her candle had plenty more wax."

Cassie pushed her lips together before a look of sadness overtook her face. "You must tend to the candle. Protect it as you protect your love. It cannot be allowed to go out before the wick is spent."

"What happens if the candle goes out?"

"Your love – the person – dies."

I looked at the basement door. "So, the person that woman loved is dead?"

Cassie nodded. "Candle magic is very dangerous. Love potions are even worse. We saw something horrible happen in Ireland. An apprentice who should not have been toying with it decided to cast a love spell on a boy she desired. He became so infatuated with her that he tried to kidnap her and ended up hurting her pretty badly. When he realized he couldn't have her, he was so stricken with loneliness and grief that he hung himself."

I shook my head. "Aunt Dori wouldn't take that kind of risk. Why would she?"

"Dorinda started this shop to help people. And she does. But all magic has risks because it changes the natural order of things. She can only continue to help people if we can afford to keep this shop open and, unfortunately, it's the darkest potions that are the most lucrative."

Just then, we heard the basement door unlock and we ducked low behind the shelf. We peeked over the top and watched Dori escort the woman outside. At once, we made a mad dash back to our stations. Cassie pretended to be looking at her spreadsheet while I pretended to stock shelves.

Dori came back in, shaking her head. "So tragic." She didn't even make eye contact with us as she returned to the basement below.

I glanced over to Cassie. She was forcing herself to stare at the computer screen and refusing to make eye contact with me.

Cassie carried on the next few days as if nothing had ever been said and neither of us told Aunt Dori that I knew her secret. But I dwelled on that secret. Magic wasn't real. Was it? Cassie and Aunt Dori had been so serious about the candle burning out and the woman had indeed been crying over someone who died. I found myself watching the basement door and the comings and goings of the shop more closely. Most people seemed to be normal clients with normal ailments. People who needed something to help them sleep, or migraine relief, weight loss, or a relative had a head cold. Aunt Dori helped them all with a broad smile and since she had been training me, I assisted people when she was busy. But every so often, she would bring a sealed box from the basement for Cassie to ship with the other online orders or I would see her discreetly escort someone who had an appointment through the door and down the stairs. I found myself staring at that door. I desperately needed to know what was really going on down there.

One Sunday, late in August, I had my chance. Cassie had gone into town to go to the library. Aunt Dorinda was fussing over the state of one of her rose bushes. I told her I wanted to go do some shopping and she sent me on my way with her blessing. Before I left, I slipped her shop keys into my purse. I hopped into her old '67 Beetle and drove to the shop.

I had been in that store alone a thousand times but it never felt like this. The instant aroma of the dried fennel and rosemary sachets over the front door greeted me. I could smell every herb and taste the alcohol in some of the tinctures in the air. It seemed dark despite the sunlight pouring through the windows. I set my purse on the counter and removed Aunt Dori's keys.

The basement key was small and brass. It felt warm in my fingers. I put my hand on the doorknob and felt myself shudder. It felt wrong to betray Aunt Dori's trust. She had once told me that I would know what was down there when she was ready for me to know. But I wasn't a child anymore and she had given no indication that she was going to come clean any time soon. I suddenly became aware that I was grinding my teeth as I contemplated what I was doing. I steeled myself and turned the key in the lock. My heart jumped a little when I heard the click of the latch. I opened the door to darkness. Immediately to my right, I saw a light switch. I flipped it and saw a soft glow appear below.

I descended the stairs into a poorly lit room about half the size of the shop. The walls were a dark forest green color. The air smelled moist but without mildew. In the center of the room was an oak coffee table in between a beige loveseat and a brown armchair. The rug under the furniture looked odd and I realized on further inspection that it was a large patch of live moss. Around the room were a few strange-looking potted plants that must have naturally thrived in almost no light. To the left, half the wall was a floor-to-ceiling bookcase. Next to the bookcase was a door and on the wall opposite the stairs was a kitchenette.

I approached the small kitchen space. There was a kettle on the gas stove and what looked like gingerbread cookies in a jar. I opened the cabinets and drawers. I found some of my Auntie's favorite teas, pots, pans, wooden spoons, mortar and pestle, and other things you would expect to find. I ventured to the bookcase. The bottom shelves were tomes and textbooks she had collected in her studies. The upper shelves appeared to be her notebooks from her travels. I pulled down a few and flipped through them casually. Each was labeled with the year, the country she was in, and, in some cases, the Indigenous peoples she was learning from. They contained notes, rubbings of plants, and hand-drawn diagrams.

I put the notebooks back on the shelves. I sighed a bit

and looked around. How silly could I have been? It was just a little office with a space to make tea for her clients. Granted, the live moss rug was weird. What had I been expecting to find? Eye of newt and tongue of dog? A cauldron simmering over a fire? I laughed at myself and glanced at the other door. It was probably a closet but I opened it anyway, still giggling at myself. It was not a closet.

There were shelves and shelves of jars and containers. One shelf held various colored blocks of wax, presumably to make candles. Other shelves contained oils derived from plants and labeled with Latin names. There were jars containing pig bile, feathers from multiple species of birds, chalk dust, salts, more dried plants labeled in languages I couldn't read, and a multitude of bugs, both dead and alive. Some shelves had pots made of different materials, iron, copper, steel, and even a few bowls that looked suspiciously like the tops of skulls. There were curved knives, straight ones, and serrated ones next to empty jars and vials with blank labels awaiting contents.

I looked around and tried to absorb everything. It was real. I didn't know that I believed in magic, but my sweet, tea-making, salt-of-the-earth Auntie was a witch. I returned to the office room and pulled the door closed behind me. I looked back at the bookshelves. I selected a few of the notebooks that I hoped she wouldn't notice were gone. Back at the top of the stairs, I tucked the notebooks in my purse. I don't know what compelled me, but I knew I needed to know more about what was really going on down there. On the way home, I stopped by the market to corroborate my cover story.

Over the following months, things seemed to be normal at the shop but I started seeing it all in new light. I realized that Cassie wasn't just haggling with vendors when she took her foreign calls; she was vetting wealthy potential clients in need of potions and spells. At night alone, in my room, I read through the journals and Googled many of the ingredients in her notes. More than half of them were considered poisons in high doses. Night sweats, liver failure, heart palpitations, and other problems were reported with many of the herbs. Odd as it sounds, I didn't see any difference between that and the loads of side effects listed on medication commercials. I realized just how specific the questions were that Aunt Dori had trained me to ask before making suggestions. She knew the dangers of many of her plants and wanted to make sure we provided more help than harm.

But homemade medicine was only part of her notes. In her notes from Egypt, I found notes on ancient texts about the candle magic that had broken the woman's heart. I also found it in a few notebooks containing notations from Wiccan and Pagan practices. Elemental magic from several cultures in Africa seemed similar to a few in Asia. Hoodoo was fascinating as it combined Catholicism, Native American lore, African Gods, and roots, herbs, and animal fluids. The one consistency throughout every continent, faith, and practice, was the sacrifice. The strongest and most powerful spells required blood or more.

Every few weeks I would sneak away and switch out the notebooks in the basement. I was almost caught once when Aunt Dori said she couldn't find her keys. I hadn't been able to return them to her so I pretended to find them under the sofa. I don't think Cassie believed me.

As I gleaned more from Dori's notes than I did from her

training, I became more confident when speaking to customers. Cassie, who noticed everything, seemed to be suspicious. I confirmed her suspicions the following February. Aunt Dori escorted a client out of the basement and to the register where Cassie stood at the ready and I was handing off a bag of willow bark and licorice root to a congested client.

"Ms. Abernathy will be needing this." She set a long, purple box on the counter. "And the small conifer on the right." She indicated the potted evergreen to the side of the front door.

Ms. Abernathy dabbed her eyes with a tissue and reached into her purse for her wallet.

"Perhaps some Ashwagandha to help with the stress?" I suggested.

"Excellent idea," Dori beamed at me. "Give her two weeks' worth at no extra charge."

Cassie gave me a sideways look as I turned to measure the powder into a sealable bag with a label. Ms. Abernathy put the purple box and the Ashwagandha in her purse and she and Dori loaded the little evergreen into a red car.

"That's such a shame. I really liked that little tree," I said as I watched them.

"It was a good sale," Cassie countered.

"Yeah, but now it's going to die." Cassie turned and looked at me. "It's a put-away tree, isn't it? Bortsättningsträd. You and Dori have been raising those little trees so people can transfer illness into them."

"So, you have been going into the basement. Reading Dorinda's notes." Cassie turned to face me with the accusation.

"You two left me no choice."

"I knew I shouldn't have told you anything." She began

wringing her hands. "Dorinda is going to be so mad when she finds out."

"How is she going to find out?" I asked. "I have no intention of telling her and I know *you* aren't going to tell her."

"Why are you doing this?" she asked.

"I want to understand. I want to know."

"You aren't trying to cast any spells, are you?" Her face was grave.

"Don't be ridiculous. Auntie Dori has been studying this stuff with people who actually practice it for decades. I've been reading notes for a few months."

"Promise?" she asked.

"I promise. I just want to understand."

Cassie looked a little relieved, but still ill at ease.

Over the next few months, the bitter cold rolling off of Lake Michigan gave way and the perpetual cloud cover of winter parted to a cool, bright sunlight. Cassie and I were spring cleaning around the shop. Spiders were welcome in the winter because they are signs of wealth and prosperity and they need a warm place to stay. In the spring, however, they had to be evicted and their webs cleared. Dust accumulated on the uppermost shelves where we kept the rarely used ingredients that required a ladder to reach.

I took a glass jar off of a shelf and began to dust it. "When was the last time we recommended Brahmi tea?" I asked Cassie.

"It's been a while. It's so bitter and you burp up the taste for hours after you take it. People don't care how well it works with a side effect like that."

I giggled and returned the jar to the shelf. I heard the light bell on the door jingle and turned. A tall, broad-shouldered man with sandy hair wearing a blue sweater and khakis stood in the doorway. He looked around the small space, his pale blue eyes wide with wonder.

"How can we help you?" Aunt Dori greeted him.

"Oh, um." The man looked down at her as if suddenly realizing he wasn't alone. "The homeopathy shop up the road said I might have better luck here," he said.

"Homeopathy," Aunt Dori muttered. "Such utter nonsense. What can a real herbalist help you with?"

The man cocked a crooked smile. "My mom hasn't really been feeling herself lately. She's not sleeping and she's grouchy. She's tried chamomile and valerian but it's not helping and she doesn't want to just keep knocking herself out with allergy medicine because she doesn't get any rest even though she sleeps. She asked if I could try to find something while I was out shopping today."

Aunt Dori nodded her head knowingly and guided him by the shoulder further into the shop. "And probably around my age, too?" she asked.

"Uh—"

"It's alright. I'm not old; I've just been around for a while." The man smiled weakly. "Cassie, where's that green tea that came in last week?"

Cassie, realizing she was staring at the handsome stranger, blinked and pointed at a large jar on the shelf below me.

"Ah, yes," said Aunt Dori. "Thank you. I think it will have an adequate theanine content as it's fresh. We'll need to mix it two parts to one part black cohosh powder." She looked thoughtful for a moment. "Better throw in one part Tulsi leaves as well."

"I understood 'green tea,'" said the man.

"That's okay Mr.?"

"Ezra. Just Ezra."

"Lovely, Hebrew name. It means 'helper.'" Aunt Dori smiled. "And here you are helping your mother."

"This is an amazing place you have here," Ezra said.

"Thank you, Dear. Why don't I show you around a bit."

As Aunt Dori gave her tour, I climbed down my ladder and began combining the ingredients as instructed. Cassie had stationed herself behind the register inputting the ingredients into a client profile for when this elegant man would inevitably return for more. It had the added advantage of being able to see almost all corners of the shop so she could subtly observe him. And, I couldn't help but notice, that her usual tight bun had come down and her long, black hair was falling down her back.

Aunt Dori and Ezra returned to the counter. I handed him the bag of mixed ingredients. Our fingers lightly brushed and I felt a little electric shock. My face got hot and I knew I was blushing fiercely, but he only smiled at me.

Aunt Dori, seemingly oblivious, started barking instructions. "Boil water and let it cool to two hundred degrees. Steep two measured teaspoons in six ounces of the water for three to five minutes. Make sure you keep the mug covered while steeping so the oils that would otherwise evaporate fall back into the water. Your mother may want to strain out the leaves before drinking. Oh, and I recommend a teaspoon of honey; these ingredients may be a bit bitter."

"I have no idea how I'm going to remember all of that," Ezra admitted.

Cassie flashed a piece of paper in front of him. "I wrote it down. And our phone number if your mom has any questions."

Ezra took the proffered paper. "Thank you, very much."

I giggled silently to myself. Cassie had written the instructions on our stationery. The stationery had the shop's address and phone number printed with the logo but it was her cell phone number handwritten at the bottom for him to call.

After he had paid and left, I fell over myself laughing. "Cassie and Ezra sitting in a tree…" I sang.

She hurled a dirty dustcloth at me. "As if you didn't look like a blonde tomato when you handed him his tea."

A month later, the handsome Ezra returned. "My mother would love some more of that tea you made for her. She's been feeling wonderful!"

"I'm so glad!" Aunt Dori met him at the door. "Now, let's get you something for your tummy troubles while the girls put your order together." She began to guide him toward the front window case.

"How did you know?" He looked at her in bewilderment as she led him away.

I looked over at Cassie. Her bun had once again vanished and she was pulling up the ingredients we had used to make his tea in her index. I rolled my eyes and went to retrieve jars of green tea, Tulsi leaves, and black cohosh powder. As I turned from the shelf, I bumped into Ezra, nearly dropping the heavy glass jars. He reached out and helped me steady them.

"Are you okay?" he asked.

"Yes. Thank you." I smiled. "I'm just a bit clumsy."

"Are you a student at the university?"

"No. My Auntie owns the shop and I help her run it full time."

He nodded thoughtfully. "Do you like it here?"

"Very much. Aunt Dori has taught me a lot. And I get to help people every day. It's not that different from any other pharmacy."

He helped me set the jars on the counter so I could begin to measure the ingredients. He handed an orange pouch to Cassie. "Is Dori your aunt too?" he asked.

"No. She's my guardian." Cassie pulled her hair over her shoulder and began running her fingers through it. This was a behavior that surfaced when she was truly nervous, which was why it was always in a bun.

"Guardian?" he asked.

"Yes. I was an orphan when I was four. Dorinda adopted me on one of her trips and I have traveled the world with her ever since."

"And you?" Ezra turned to me. "How did you come to be here?"

"Also an orphan," I admitted. "My mom was Dori's niece. She and my dad died when I was ten and Dori took me in."

"Did you travel too?"

"No." I shook my head. "I was put in boarding school for a bit but I was bullied. Dori stopped traveling so I could attend public school and be normal."

Ezra turned to Dori. "You have a big heart."

"Nonsense. My shop may provide me with a living

but my girls provide me with life." She pulled us both into her sides.

After that Ezra became a regular fixture at the shop. He bought tinctures for headaches and powders for allergies. He would always come to me and ask me questions about what was in specific jars and once he even asked me why Dori had such a hatred of homeopathy. Eventually, the conversations turned away from the shop and powders and poultices. He asked me about books and movies and what kind of food I liked. He even brought a few of his friends with him to show them around and Dori and I helped them with their ailments too. I wasn't used to such attention but I enjoyed it. Cassie stopped letting her hair down when he entered the shop. He didn't show her the same attention he showed me. I found myself thinking about him when I was alone in my room and dreaming about him at night. I could not keep from smiling when I was around him and I knew I was falling for him deeper and deeper.

While out running errands one day, I saw him sitting and having coffee with a man he had once brought into the Apothecary. I felt my heart leap and I decided to say hello. I got closer and could hear his friend talking.

"What about that cute little blonde girl at the tea shop you're always going about?'

"Nah. I like her. I really do. But I feel like she's a really good friend."

"Uh-huh." His friend took a sip of his coffee. "Then how come you're in there every other week?"

"I don't know. I just really like the place. I feel... I don't know... different when I'm in there. Like all of my worries have melted away. I'm not thinking about Mom or work or anything stressful. And all the women in there are pretty awesome but I really just don't see any of them *romantically*."

Ezra's confession cut through me. I was a good friend. He couldn't see me as a romantic partner. All this time I thought we were flirting and getting closer together was for nothing. He didn't feel the same way about me as I did about him. I turned and fled before he could see me.

That evening, I sat on my bed and cried. We had grown so close. My feelings for him were genuine and true. If I could only make him see. If he would only give me the chance to make him feel about me the way I felt about him. All I needed was time... The time it would take a candle to burn. I fought with myself over the idea. Magic was dangerous. I could kill him. What had Cassie said about a love potion that went wrong and ended in suicide? I argued with the voices in my head for hours. Finally, long after Cassie and Aunt Dori were asleep, I slipped out of the house and to the shop. I was going to see how complicated the spell would be and that would be what would convince me to give up such a crazy idea.

In Auntie's basement office, I pulled a black notebook from the very back of a very top shelf. It contained notes she had made from all over the world on a very specific subject. Candle magic. I flipped through until I found what I was looking for. It looked like a combination of Egyptian and Roman magic. I ran down the list of ingredients. I was able to locate most in Auntie's secret storage. One would be hard to find. I needed a bit of the other person. The spell seemed almost too simple otherwise. I returned the book to its place and crept home.

As I lay in bed, I wondered how I could obtain a part of Ezra. Pluck out a few of his hairs? Find out where he lived and sneak into his apartment? Each idea was more absurd than the last. I did not sleep that night.

Two days later I had my answer by accident. Ezra stopped by the shop to decompress after a long day at work. We socialized but I tried to maintain a distance. At one point I turned and tripped over my own feet. He caught me and I scratched him as I grabbed his arm.

"Are you okay?" I looked at a red line forming down his lightly freckled skin.

"Of course. It's just a scratch."

"I've got just the thing for that!" Auntie Dori appeared out of thin air and guided him away.

I looked at the nail of my middle finger. There was a faint roll of his skin trapped underneath. I had my piece of him right there in my hand. I scurried over to the desk and, using the glue part of a sticky note, removed the skin. I folded it into the paper and tucked it in my pocket before anyone could notice.

"Good as new!" I heard my aunt exclaim.

"You really do work magic, Miss Dori," Ezra said.

If only he knew.

Around three in the morning, I heard snoring from both other bedrooms and I sneaked back to the shop. I removed the black notebook and read the spell over and over. It just seemed too simple. There were no incantations. It didn't need to be performed on a full moon. None of the things that Hollywood had trained me to expect were necessary.

I wondered if I should really attempt it. I wondered if I

should just talk to Dori and have her perform the spell for me. At least then I would know it was done right. No. Dori would never do it for me. She didn't even want me to know about this place or what she did down here. But I loved him. With all my heart, I loved him. I just needed him to realize that he could love me too.

I turned on the gas stove in the little kitchenette. I put a copper pot on it and began to melt the beeswax. Into the wax was mixed bovine tallow (enough to make it turn yellow), jasmine petals, mandragora leaves, blue Nile lily blossoms, green apple seeds, and powder of ground scarabs. When it was all mixed into the wax, I added the paper containing his skin. Lastly, I sealed the spell with a bit of my own blood by puncturing my thumb with the point of a gold-tipped blade. I chose a wick and the largest candle mold I could find. I wanted to make sure I had ample time for Ezra to fall in love with me. I poured the wax into the mold and as it cooled, I cleaned and tidied everything. Auntie Dori could never know I was here.

When I returned to my room, I set the candle on my dresser in front of the mirror and stared at it. Had I done everything right? Was I really prepared to do this? To an extent, I was taking away his free will. I was influencing him unnaturally. But it was for the right reasons. I knew it was.

I held my breath as I lit the candle. The yellow flame from the lighter turned a bold blue as soon as it touched the wick. There was no going back.

The next day Ezra bounded into the shop after work. He took my hands into his. "Have dinner with me Saturday night?"

There was no greeting of the day or even coy behavior but there was a pleading I had never seen in his eyes before.

"Of course," I said.

Aunt Dori clapped her hands together. "It's about time!"

On Saturday he picked me up from the shop and we went to a lovely Italian restaurant in uptown. I hadn't been on a date since high school and I was admittedly very nervous. I ordered a glass of wine as we talked. At one point I reached for the wine and knocked it over, staining the white tablecloth.

"What the Hell?" he exclaimed.

"I'm sorry. Did it get on you?"

"No. If it had you *would* be sorry."

I was too stunned by his outburst to speak. We finished dinner at a different table in relative silence. When he dropped me off at the shop after dinner, we stood in front of the door to say goodnight.

"I'm sorry I snapped," he said. He sounded sincere but I didn't let my guard down. "I really don't know what came over me." He kissed the back of my hand.

"It's...it's okay," I managed to say.

He smiled halfheartedly and nodded once before returning to his car.

When I returned home, I had expected Aunt Dori and Cassie to be waiting to hear all of the juicy gossip, but neither one of them was still up. I went to my room and closed the door. The candle's flame flickered an eerie blue, taunting me in the darkness.

Three days later he returned to the shop. "I'm sorry, I had

to see you again. I can't stop thinking about you. You'll go out with me again this weekend."

I had had several days to think about it. I wasn't sure I wanted to continue pursuing something romantic with Ezra after his behavior. Maybe he wasn't who I thought he was. I didn't like the way he had said I *would* be sorry. I had decided to let the candle burn out without actively trying to make him fall in love with me. It pained me and my feelings were still there, but something told me it wasn't right.

"I don't think so. You're a nice guy and all but I just think we're better friends."

His pale blue eyes darkened. "You didn't hear me." He grabbed my arm around the top of my bicep. "You *will* go out with me again this weekend."

I looked desperately at the desk. Cassie was still out dropping packages off to be shipped and Aunt Dori was in the basement where she couldn't hear me.

He squeezed tighter.

"Ow! Okay!" I heard myself yelp.

His grip released and his eyes softened. He smiled. "Excellent! I'll pick you up at 730 on Saturday night!"

As I watched him glide out the door as if on a cloud, I started grinding my teeth. Should I tell Dori? She was just downstairs. No. Then she would know what I had done. She would be so disappointed in me. I could handle this.

On Saturday night he, again, picked me up from the shop. I wasn't keen on the idea of letting him know where we lived. All of my muscles were locked and tense. I let him do most of the talking throughout dinner and as we walked and talked after, I kept my arms wrapped around myself but he didn't seem to notice. The evening went off without incident. Almost. When we returned to the shop, he leaned in to kiss me but I backed away from him out of pure reflex. Once again, I saw his face morph into something angry and unrecognizable. I felt a sharp sting and tasted blood as his hand came across my face. His tires squealed as he pulled off the street and away from the shop.

I looked in the rearview mirror of the Beetle and saw a little split in my lip. I cried. What had I done? I cried the entire drive home. I reminded myself how stupid and foolish I had been to attempt a love spell on my own. Hadn't Cassie warned me?

In the driveway, I pulled myself together enough to walk inside the house. The living room was dark except for the light of the TV screen. Cassie was in her pajamas and watching a movie with a big tub of popcorn in her lap.

"How was your date?" she called. "Oh my God!" Her voice turned from playful to concerned as I entered the living room and she saw my lip. "What happened?"

"Where's Aunt Dori?" I asked.

"At the Parson's playing cards. What happened?" she asked again.

I broke down sobbing again. I told her everything. I told her about his outburst on our first date and about him slapping me for not kissing him. And I told her about the candle.

Her eyes bulged. "You didn't. Please, tell me you didn't."

I shook my head, unable to voice anymore.

"Show me the candle," she demanded.

I led her to my room and pointed to the dresser.

"Oh, no! You put it in front of a mirror? Why would you *do* that?" she shrieked.

"Is that bad?" I asked.

"*Bad?* What does a mirror do? It reflects light. What is a magic candle? It's magic light and you're *reflecting* it. Oh, this is bad. This is very bad."

"What does it do?"

"It either intensifies the magic because it is reflecting the light and in essence producing more or it reverses the magic because the magic imparts its effect *from* the reflected light instead of the candle. Oh, this is bad. This is very bad." She was shaking her head. "Think. Did you do anything else? Did you follow the spell exactly?"

"Yes. Exactly." Then I remembered. "Uh, oh," I said more softly.

"What did you do?"

"His skin. It was stuck to the glue of a sticky note so I threw in the whole paper."

"Paper?!" she almost screamed the word. "You introduced something UNNATURAL to the wax? Oh, shit. Shit. Shit. Shit."

I had never heard Cassie use a swear word before and it terrified me.

"What can we do?" I asked.

"Well, we can't put the candle out. It'll kill him, for sure. Why did you make such a big candle?"

"I wanted to make sure he would have time to fall in love with me," I admitted quietly.

"Well, now we have to wait that long for it to burn out and

keep you safe in the meantime. We'll need to talk to Dorinda about what else we can do."

"No. Aunt Dori can never find out about this! She'll never trust me again! She'll never trust either of us!"

"What did I do?" Cassie asked indignantly. "YOU made the candle."

"YOU told me what was going on in the basement against her wishes."

Cassie pursed her lips together. "Fine."

"What are we going to do now?"

"Now? Now we're going down to the police station and filing an assault charge. Maybe we can get him locked up until the candle burns out or at least buy you some time."

I reluctantly agreed and she drove me to the station. It was a fruitless effort. The officer took my statement but said because it was 'only a split lip' and I had no proof Ezra did it or witnesses, he couldn't press charges. I was crestfallen as I went to bed that night.

Over the next few weeks, Ezra tried to corner me again. I knew what time he got off of work through the week and I would make excuses to run errands, drop off the packages, or get a snack at the deli. If I were in the shop, Cassie and I would watch for his car and I would hide in the cabinet under the register. Cassie would make excuses that I was out or not feeling well. It worked the first few times but he was getting angrier with every visit. He began ignoring her protestations and hunted through the shelves to see if I was hiding between them. On one visit, he flipped a table of oils and Dori told him he was no longer welcome in her shop.

When he had left, she turned to us. "I don't know what

you girls are keeping from me, but I have a feeling you know what that was about."

"I don't want to date him anymore. He isn't taking it well." My answer wasn't a complete lie.

She nodded. "Well, with a temper like that, I don't blame you." She stormed off to get a mop bucket.

It was another month and the candle still burned though it was decidedly shorter. We hadn't seen or heard from Ezra and Cassie and I unwisely let our guard down. It was after dark in the fall. I had stayed late alone to stock shelves after a particularly large shipment had arrived from Nepal. I was leaving and turned to put my key in the door to lock it. That was when I felt something hit the back of my head and send my face into the door. Ezra grabbed me by the neck and threw me back into the dark shop. My hands made a splat sound as they hit the tile, breaking my fall.

"You really thought I didn't know you were in here? Did you really think you could hide from me?" His face was a mask of rage and cruelty. There was no hint of the softness in the gentle blue eyes that had once captivated me.

"Ezra, I—"

"You are mine; don't you understand that?" He put his foot on my chest and shoved me to the floor. "MINE!"

I grabbed his foot and shoved it to the side, momentarily throwing him off balance. I scrambled to get away from him but he grabbed my ankle and pulled me back to him. He snatched a fistful of my hair and threw my head into the hard floor. There was a dull, sickening smack sound as my skull contacted the tile. The edges of my vision went dark while a burst of color exploded in front of my eyes.

"I think about you EVERY minute of EVERY day! I can't sleep because I want your body in the bed next to mine. I go home to an empty apartment when you should be there waiting for me. I hear your voice from across the room every day at work. I smell your soap everywhere I go! I NEED you!"

Again, I tried to get up but my vision was still flickering in and out. He put a knee on either side of me and straddled my hips. He grabbed another fist full of my hair and shoved his lips hard against mine. I never knew a kiss could be so painful. Not knowing what else to do, I bit down on his lip as hard as I could. He screamed and pulled away from me. I saw blood streaming down his chin just before my head went back against the floor, harder this time, and everything went black.

When I started to wake up, I was acutely aware that there was a heavy weight on top of me. My head was pounding and everything was blurry. There was also a terrible pain between my legs. I squeezed my eyes shut and opened them again. Still unable to see clearly in the dark, I realized the weight holding me down was Ezra. I flash of panic-induced clarity ran through me as I realized what he was doing. I reached out and somehow my hands found my keys in the darkness. I took the longest one I could feel and jammed it in his neck as hard as I could. This was just enough to break his concentration and I was able to throw my body to get him off of me. I scrambled, felt a glass jar on a bottom shelf, and threw it down on his head as hard as I could. I heard him yelp as it broke. I managed to pull myself to my feet, still unsteady, I stomped on his head a few times, hoping to knock him unconscious.

I should have called the police. I should have locked

myself in the basement and called the police or fled to one of the shops nearby that was still open. But I didn't. I couldn't think clearly. All I knew was that the only person who could help me in the end was Aunt Dori. I don't remember driving home. It was so dark and my vision was not at all clear. I burst through the front door. Cassie dropped her bag of chips when she saw me.

"Oh my god!"

"Where's Aunt Dori?" I asked breathlessly.

"It's Saturday night. She's drinking and playing cards at the Parson's. Did Ezra do this?"

As if to answer her question, we saw Ezra's bright red car peeling down the drive. He had followed me home. We were all in danger.

"He's going to kill me!" I screamed.

"Call the police!" Cassie went for her phone.

I slammed the door and deadbolted it. The top of the birdbath from the front garden sailed through the front picture window. Cassie and I screamed. Just like in a horror movie, we ran upstairs. Cassie dropped her phone as we ran but we could see Ezra walking over the broken glass and we had no time to retrieve it. We barricaded ourselves in my bedroom and jammed my desk chair under the doorknob. We heard his body hit the door and saw the door move, but it held. Again and again, he hit it, but the door was solid wood. Cassie and I were against the far wall, holding each other and crying. Suddenly, the door stopped moving and we saw a foot come through the drywall next to it. He was breaking through the wall.

"What do we do? What do we do?" I cried. I looked at the window, trying to decide if we would survive a jump.

"Blow the candle out!" Cassie screamed.

"That'll kill him!"

"He's going to kill us!"

Cassie was right. He was going to kill us if we didn't do something. I had been the one to get us into this mess. My youthful stupidity had put us in danger. I had played with something I didn't understand.

I looked at the candle. Its haunting blue flame hardly flickered despite the chaos around it. This was not how it was supposed to be. This was not what was supposed to happen. I felt a tear roll down my cheek as I took a deep breath and blew. Suddenly, aside from Cassie's whimpering, all was silent. I watched the last ember at the tip of the wick go out and I knew that it was all over.

2

This Road

    Our fates did meet
along that path,
forgotten,
And so green.

What once was worn
was then forlorn,
feral,
hardly seen.

We trod the path
our feet as one
revealing
what was between.

Happy, smiling

we built a road
stronger
than what had been.

But then I looked.
Your feet were gone.
Alone.
Lost in routine.

Do you miss me?
I yearn for you.
This road
was just a dream.

3

Disobedience

My mother died when I was about five years old. She was the purest heart anyone could possibly meet. She was a beautiful short-haired brunette with gentle blue eyes. She kept her skin soft with this wonderful stuff that smelled like peaches. I am her stark contrast. My hair is as white as snow and I have eyes like chocolate. Everyone knew we belonged together, though. On my first birthday, she gifted me with a silver heart charm. I always wore it on my necklace and she wore the matching charm on her bracelet. I always knew where she was by the jingling sound it made.

 It was just the two of us in an apartment in the heart of the city. On the weekends, she would paint my nails and do my hair or surprise me with little dresses. We would go to play at the park or visit friends. Once a month she would take me to the salon to get my hair done. I didn't particularly enjoy it, but she always fussed over how beautiful I was after. During the week, she would drop me off at daycare in the morning. I loved playing with my friends, especially Max and Bella, but I was always excited to see her in the afternoon. I would jump in her arms and excitedly tell her about my day. When we got home, she would make dinner and we would sit on the couch in front of the TV while we ate. At night she would tuck me in and kiss my head. The next morning, we would get up and do it all again. I remember her always telling me to mind my manners and do as I'm told when she would drop me off.

Our closest family was my Uncle Seth. I didn't like him at all. He lived on the family farm outside of the city. He was a scary and stern man. He never smiled. He never joked. We never played. He was always dirty and smelled bitter. And his flatulence! When we would go to his house, he stumbled around and yelled a lot. I don't think Mommy liked visiting with him. Sometimes, I would hear them arguing and she would come to get me and we would leave in a hurry. He always had this strange look on his face whenever she was close. He would lick his lips or bite at them. I didn't know what it was, but I didn't like it and I didn't think Mommy did either. His wife had disappeared but his two sons, Derek and Ethan, were awful too. They pulled my hair and tricked me into hurting myself. Once, they waited until I was taking my nap and lit firecrackers next to me. All the while they laughed and my mommy had to come to my rescue. Thankfully I only had to endure it a few times per year.

We went to visit him a few days before Mommy died. They had gotten into another huge fight and we fled back to our apartment in the city while he chased after us and threatened her. He kept calling her and she kept hanging up on him. Shortly after, things returned to normal.

Life was good and carefree but the day she died, it was like the earth stopped spinning. That fateful morning started like any other. She dropped me off at daycare and told the girl at check-in to make sure I ate my lunch. Her last words to me before she left my life were "be a good girl."

I played with my friends all day without a care in the world. But as the afternoon turned into evening, everyone's families came to get them and they went home, everyone except me. I began to get anxious. The sitters who were in charge tried to calm me and were calling the phone numbers in my file. Finally, they reached someone. It was close to closing time before *he* showed up.

He came in the front door of the daycare. I was in the big playroom, separate from the lobby, but I could see him through the windows. He said something I couldn't hear to the girls behind the counter. They gasped and shook their heads. They looked at me through the glass. They looked sad and I was worried. Where was my mom?

Seth picked me up and tucked me in the car. I was nervous. I wasn't supposed to ride in the front seat. Mommy always said I was too small and I didn't have my car seat. We sat in silence as the car pulled on to the highway and headed out of the city.

"Well, I guess I'm stuck with you now," he said at last.

I will forever remember those words and the way they stung. I didn't ask where my mom was. I was too scared. When we got to the farmhouse, he put me up in the guest bedroom. A little while later, he brought me something cold that I think was like beef stew and some water. I wasn't hungry. He nodded at me and left the door ajar behind him. He didn't speak a word to me otherwise for the rest of the night.

It stormed heavily. I remember the rain slamming against the old glass of the dilapidated house and lightning illuminating the sky for miles. Sometime after midnight, when it wasn't quite morning, I heard what I thought was a woman scream. The big blue house on the hill had goats so I decided it must have been one of the goats that was afraid of the storm. I spent most of the night crying under the bed.

In the morning, I gathered all of my courage. I pulled the door open slowly and headed down the stairs. Seth and the boys were sitting around the kitchen table.

Ethan looked at me. "When's Aunt Amy coming to get Sophie?" The tone in his voice was cold.

I stopped and sat on the bottom step.

"She's not. Y'all won't be seeing Aunt Amy anymore. She died yesterday." He looked out the window towards the storm cellar.

The boys' jaws dropped. I couldn't believe what I'd just heard.

"What happened?" Ethan pressed.

"Car accident."

Two words. Two very plain, simple words brought my world crashing down around me. That's what he had meant by 'stuck with me.' I was going to live with him forever. I was heartbroken and terrified. I was never again going to see my mother's smile. I would never lay against her soft skin that smelled like peaches or go on our weekend adventures together. I was crushed. I ran back up the stairs and curled up on the bed.

After a few hours of crying and sleeping, my stomach forced me to get up and go back downstairs. The whole house was empty. The floorboards creaked under the weight of my tiny bare feet. The remnants of breakfast were still on the table. With no one around to help me, I pulled myself up into a chair and picked at what was left of the toaster waffles and bacon. One of the boys had left half a glass of milk and I washed it all down with that. It was awful, but I was hungry.

After I'd eaten what I could choke down, I pushed open the screen door and stepped out onto the porch. The sky was grey and heavy. I ventured off the porch and into the yard. Everything was wet from the storm. The mud squished between my toes and I hated every bit of it. I sniffed a dandelion as I carefully squatted in the grass and surveyed my surroundings. I could hear the neighbor's goats a few pastures over. Seth's hogs were out behind the barn and chickens chased each other all around me. I truly hated it there. It was dirty and smelly. I wanted my clean apartment. I wanted carpet under my feet, not grass. I wanted pavement, not mud. I wanted the city sounds of traffic below, not tractors and horses in the distance.

I heard a strange noise coming from the root cellar. I ventured closer and listened carefully. The doors flew open and Seth popped out of the ground.

"What are you doing over here?" He yelled angrily. "The cellar is out of bounds!"

I panicked and ran towards the kitchen. I ran past Derek as he was coming out of the house. I have no idea where he came from but I saw the open door and I ran through it. I ran up the stairs and cowered back in my bed.

"Don't go near the cellar!" Derek yelled after me.

That night, Seth came into my room with another bowl of some canned-type meat that wasn't fit for the hogs and some water.

He glowered at me from the doorway. "You can't stay in this room forever. You either come down and start interacting with the family or I'm gonna drop you in the woods out back and let you fend for yourself. Only reason I'm letting you stay here at all is out of respect for my sister." He turned and left.

I picked at the meat and thought about what he'd said. I didn't think he would really leave me in the woods by myself but I didn't trust that he wouldn't either. I thought about my mommy. I imagined smelling her peaches and curling up in her arms in front of the TV. I started to cry.

Then I heard her voice. *"Mind your manners and do as you're told. Be a good girl."*

Okay, Mommy. I'll be good.

The next morning started the year of Hell. I came down for breakfast with the family. It was awkward and uncomfortable. I didn't know where to sit. The food was awful. The boys were loud and complaining. The school bus passed the house and they grabbed their bags and ran after it.

Seth stood up and walked towards the front door. "Don't get into trouble." He swung the screen door and was gone. That was it. No daycare. No kiss goodbye on the head. The kitchen table was left a mess. This was my life now.

Seth didn't help me brush my hair or take me to the salon so it got dirty and matted. The knots tugged at my skin and hurt. He eventually took his beard trimmer and buzzed my hair down like one of the boys. I was mortified and looked awful when he was done. He didn't trim or paint my nails so I resorted to biting them off when they got too long. He never brought my things from the apartment so I had no toys of my own to play with. I didn't dare play with Ethan or Derek's toys. When they would play with me, they would set the rooster after me and watch me run from him. They also liked to throw balls at me- not *to* me- *at* me when I wasn't looking.

I missed my friends at daycare. Most days I wandered around the farm to keep myself busy or I napped in the grass. I eventually got comfortable with the new smells and sounds out there. The hens kept their distance from me. The hogs were fat and happy. They'll eat anything but whatever that special feed Seth made them smelled awful and they loved it. There were always birds and butterflies to watch on lazy days. But at night it was a little scarier. That old house creaked and groaned with every blowing wind. I could hear things scurrying around inside the walls. Some nights, I could swear I heard screaming outside. A few times, I was brave enough to peek out the window and I could see Seth coming out of the forbidden cellar wiping his hands with a rag.

This cycle of torment from the boys during the day and screams at night went on for about a year. But I never fought back and I never asked about the screams or smells from the cellar. I came down for breakfast every morning. I came in for dinner every night. I choked down the awful stews and meats with soggy vegetables I was served for dinner. I went to bed on time and without a fuss. I was a good girl. I did as I was told.

One summer day, I was out chasing butterflies. I had nothing better to do but I wasn't paying attention and chased a particularly big blue one right past the cellar. I heard a moaning noise and stopped in my tracks when I realized where I was. I listened. I heard the noise again. I looked around and didn't see Seth or the boys.

To this day, I don't know what possessed me to do it. I managed to lift the heavy door up just enough to squeeze my little body through. It was dark and wet down there and smelled of putrid blood and meat. There was just enough light coming through the crack in the cellar doors to see a few feet in front of me. I could see the silhouette of something big- like an adult- moving on a steel table against the far wall. That seemed to be where the moaning was coming from. I started to move closer but the glint of something shiny on the other wall caught my eye. I moved towards the sparkling object. The smell of decay got stronger but mixed with another smell... peaches.

There was my mother – what was left of her - laying on a bed of dead flowers. He'd kept her body down there the whole time. I didn't know how he'd gotten her or why he had her, but her rotting remains were right in front of me. The charm bracelet was just as shiny as the last time I'd seen her. I gripped it carefully and tried to pull it off her wrist. Some of the rotted flesh came with it. Just as it slid over the remnants of her hand, the cellar doors flew open.

"What are you doing down here?!" Seth was red-faced breathing heavy.

In that split second, I made a choice. I ran. I bolted up

the steps and between Seth's legs. I sprinted as fast as my legs could carry me across the field.

Seth tried to follow me but he was old and overweight. "Stop! Sophie! Come back here!" Each word sounded like it was further and further behind me. "Bad dog! Sophie! Come back here!"

I had never disobeyed like this before. I didn't know what he would do if I had stopped and gone back, and I didn't want to know. I just kept running as fast as my little legs could carry me. I ran towards the sound of the neighbor's goats. They were the nearest people I knew of. Hopefully, they would help me.

I almost got lost in the cornfield as I headed towards the pastures. I ran past the horses, the barn, and the goats. I was so relieved when I saw the big, blue house. I ran up the porch steps and collapsed from exhaustion in front of the door.

I heard a woman's voice. "Hey, little doggy. Where did you come from?" I felt her pick me up. "What do you have here?" I felt her take the bracelet from between my teeth. I tried to flip my head so she could see the same charm on my necklace. "Is… is that blood? Jack! Call the police!"

It was a few days before they tracked the bracelet back to Uncle Seth. I don't know what happened to the woman who was tied to the butcher table or my mommy's remains. I heard the lady, whose name was Tammy, saying that they found evidence of a lot of women being kept down in that cellar and killed down there. They said he'd admitted to killing my mommy but didn't have the heart to dispose of her. How did he dispose of the rest? The hogs, of course.

Tammy wasn't quite my mommy. She didn't paint my nails

or take me to the salon or daycare, but she did brush my hair every night. She gave me good meals for dinner and let me sit on her lap and watch TV. She said I was the bravest little dog she ever knew and she and Jack were glad to have a good little girl like me.

4

The Witness

There was a flutter in the hayloft. In that moment, I knew this time there had been a witness.

My little farm wasn't much. It was situated on the western edge of Appalachia in Southern Ohio. Where most people in this area dedicated their acreage to the standard corn and soybean rotation, I chose to breed a variety and sell to farmer's markets and small niche businesses that marketed organic and local-grown wares or ingredients. I had around fifty hens and a handful of roosters. Eggs were plentiful and sold to the restaurants and local people as well. Big Daddy, the king of the roost, kept the younger cocks in line and defended the flock from foxes and the occasional mink. I had a heifer named Adelaide who was allowed to calf every other year and I sold her excess milk to a man who made artisan cheese (whatever that is) up the road. I had two miniature horses- one dapple and one black- named Max and Noah. They earned their keep by pulling a cart full of produce, supplies, or even me. They were prepared for whatever was needed for the day's activity. Harriet, the old mule, was allowed to stay because, after nearly thirty years together, I owed her a comfortable retirement. Six sows and a boar yielded one to two hundred piglets per year. It wasn't much, but I raised them farrow to finish. This meant more time and labor, but more profit for each. I had three Nubian goats. I sold their milk to the same weirdo up the road for cheese and their kids to children as 4-H projects. Two turkeys per year made Christmas and Thanksgiving and sometimes I'd have ducks if the market price looked like it would be good that year. Of course, there were plenty of cats to keep the vermin at bay. A border collie named Dewey rounded off my animal menagerie by keeping the other animals in line and alerting us to danger.

A good portion of the land was set aside for raising corn, oats, and hay. Some was sold but most of it was meant to feed my own animals. The apple orchard brought tourists and money every fall. My market produce included zucchini, spaghetti squash, broccoli, carrots, corn, tomatoes, and romaine lettuce. But the one thing that attracted everyone to my booth every summer was my strawberries. They were huge, bright, and bursting with flavor.

When the farm had originally belonged to my grandparents, they were corn growers, just like their neighbors, with a small plot to grow food for the family, a few sheep, and Harriet. They had a big Anatolian shepherd named Shep who guarded the flock. On his last night on duty, he successfully defended the lambs from a hungry bobcat that had moved into the area. Unfortunately, though he did hold the assailant at bay long enough for Grandpa to come out and shoot it, Shep was suffering from his own wounds and Grandpa had to turn the gun on him too. We all cried as we laid him to rest under the strawberry patch. The following summer, the fruit grew bigger and fuller than ever before. Grandma said it was his last gift to us for loving him so much. After that, any animal that died on the farm, be it a lamb, barn cat, or goldfish was given a respectful burial under the strawberries.

I loved my grandparents and I loved that farm. Every summer was spent with them and in those fields. Grandpa and I meticulously monitored the crop and tended to the animals. He taught me to respect- not fear- the snakes in the hay bales and the owl in the loft. He said they were important workers on the farm too because they helped keep the vermin out of the feed and crops. I loved the owl. Her moon-white face in contrast to her dark brown body was beautiful. Some nights, when the light from the moon was just right, I'd catch a glimpse of her silently soaring past the bats. The snakes, however, liked to startle me. I neither found this amusing nor did I find them attractive. Despite them, the farm was my slice of Heaven on Earth.

My parents shipped my brother and me over from our home in West Virginia a week after school let out in the summer and we came home a week before school started in the fall. While I looked forward to it every year, my brother, on the other hand, hated everything about rural life. He chose to view our summers on the farm as punishment. He wasn't entirely wrong. My brother was prone to making the wrong friends and finding mischief with them. He bullied me mercilessly for being short and having red hair. Once, he went so far as to shave my head and told me that maybe I could grow a soul now. Do you have any idea how traumatizing it is for a second-grade girl to be bald? I remember looking down at my bloody knuckles after I had gone blind with rage and beaten him unforgivingly.

He wasn't always that extreme, but the torment was brutal. Truth be told, I've always had a volatile temper and he knew just how to trigger it when he was bored. On the farm, rather than helping, he remained in the house. He slept until noon, played video games until supper, then stayed up all night barricaded in his room. It kept him away from me, so I didn't mind. He swore every day at supper that as soon as he turned eighteen, he was off to New York or Seattle and he was leaving this (unpleasant word) hole behind. The day he moved out for good, I celebrated.

Over the years, I stopped only going to the farm in the summers and after high school, I moved in full-time. My grandparents were aged and had difficulty keeping up. There was less profit from the corn coming in so some of the help had to be let go. I did the best I could to fill in, but the farm was steadily declining. I was twenty years old when the unthinkable happened and my grandparents were killed in a car accident.

My brother was twenty-two at the time. He hadn't made it to Seattle yet, only as far as Cincinnati. He had completely cut contact with the family when he moved out. I didn't miss him. I had assumed he was dead in a ditch from a drug overdose. When they died, my mother hired a private investigator to track him down and tell him when and where the funeral was.

To this day, I'm not sure why Grandma and Grandpa left the farm to *both* of us. Maybe, it was out of some sense of obligation. They felt like they had to leave at least *something* to him. I didn't think it was fair. I had worked my fingers to the bone on the farm since childhood. It was mine in every way but the deed.

They weren't even in the ground yet before he started talking about how much we would get when we sold it. I reminded him that it was half mine and I was not selling. This resulted in a screaming match next to the graves. My hatred for him resurfaced and again, I lashed out, my fists landing blow after blow and his knee buckled after a particularly swift kick. Our parents, who sided with me (which only enraged him more), pulled us apart and kept us separated for the remainder of the day.

That night, he found me in the barn. I was sitting on an old tack trunk, sobbing over the loss of my family. My heartache meant nothing to him. He was soulless and cruel. Initially feigning sympathy, he again started talking about the "old dump." He told me not to be unreasonable. He picked the wrong place and more so, the wrong time to rekindle the fight. My emotions were already running high from the last week's events and I had barely kept them in check for the sake of my parents. But that was the final straw. He took me from feeling blue to seeing red. I unleashed two decades of anger, hatred, hurt, and everything in between. The resulting battle was more visceral than any we had ever had before. And I hit him. Hard. He fell back with a look of shock and disbelief on his face.

More quickly than it had come, the rage left me. I looked

to Heaven for guidance, knowing my grandparents were looking down in disapproval. In a fleeting moment of absent-mindedness, I noticed the owl was not in her roost. I looked out the open barn door and saw a purple night that was full of stars.

I didn't see my brother again for more than ten years. It would take another death to bring us back together. Most everyone assumed he had returned to his life in the city without contact again. I didn't care. He didn't come after me for the farm or try to sell it out from under me and that was all that mattered.

Over the next few years, I allowed some of the largest equipment to be repossessed and sold others. This was how the farm became so diversified. Without the large equipment, I needed something I could manage with a small tractor and minimal help. I repurposed most of the land and expanded the strawberry patch. Once I had the farm certified as organic, the money became much better. It took some time, but I eventually created something sustainable and I was happy.

The weekdays were spent toiling and working with the local businesses. The weekends (for two seasons of the year) were spent at the farmer's markets to sell the excess produce. Whatever was left on Monday went to a small grocer about forty miles away that sold smoothies and organic fruits and vegetables to yuppies from the city. Other than my animals and a handful of friends, my life was a fairly solitary one.

On the Ninth of July, just before my thirtieth birthday, I was sitting at my booth at the farmer's market and working on a crossword puzzle. It was a sticky, hot day. It had been busy but uneventful earlier. The afternoon rush was winding down and some of the other people were packing up early, being driven off by the heat. A shadow cast over my table. Assuming it was a cloud, I didn't bother to look up until it spoke.

"I was told this was the place to come for strawberries," it said.

Slightly startled, I looked up. The suspected cloud that had cast the shadow was, in fact, a *very* large man. He was well over six feet tall and more than half as wide, with a little bit of a belly in the middle. His thick brown beard was well groomed and trimmed in stark contrast to the messy mop of matching curls on top of his head. His dingy white t-shirt was drenched with sweat and his well-formed muscles threatened the seams of the sleeves. Clutched in his hands was a faded and frayed red ball cap. Clear blue eyes sparkled above a wide, toothy grin.

Forgetting that I had been balancing on two legs on my chair, I fell backward and hit the ground with a thud.

"Are you okay?" He shuffled around to the back of the booth and lifted me to my feet with ease.

Feeling more than slightly embarrassed, I tried to smile. "Oh, yes. I'm fine. Momma always said it was a good thing she didn't name me Grace."

He chuckled. "Well, Not-Grace, I'm Josh." He held out this hand.

"Most people call me Andi." I put my hand in his. It completely engulfed mine.

"Okay, Andi. Do you have any strawberries left?"

"I'm sorry," I said. "I sold out a couple of hours ago."

His exceedingly masculine features became crestfallen.

"Darn it. They were for my niece's birthday party Sunday. I can get 'em from the grocery but I wanted something special. Everybody says this was the place to come."

"No need for flattery." I put my hand on his hairy forearm. "You had me at 'birthday.'"

"What do you mean?" He brightened a little.

"You know the green farmhouse with the orchard on the bend of Rosewood Road?"

"Yes, ma'am. The Birmingham farm."

Hearing my grandparents' name stung a little, but I refused to let it show. "I'm their granddaughter. Strawberries are best picked after the dew is lifted but before the heat so be at the back door tomorrow morning at nine and bring a basket."

His face lit up like a Christmas tree. "Thank you! Thank you, so much!" His hand swallowed mine once more as he shook it hard enough to throw me off balance. He turned and almost skipped toward the parking lot.

The next morning, right on time, I saw a dust cloud headed down my long dirt drive. He parked his red truck next to my blue one. He hopped out of the driver's seat wearing the faded red hat, a clean, grey t-shirt that was, again, stretched to the limit at the sleeves, blue jeans, and that big, toothy smile. In his hands, he held a wicker basket with pink, frilly lace around the edges. The sight made me giggle a little.

"Mornin'," I called as I approached from the shed, Dewey running ahead to greet the stranger.

"Mornin'," he said back as he crouched to pet the border collie. "Can't tell you how much I appreciate this."

"It's no trouble. Can't have Uncle Josh be a liar, now, can we?"

As I spoke, he stood and I suddenly became aware that I was maybe a third of his size. It was an intimidating realization and I suddenly wondered if the Ruger 380 I had tucked in a holster in my pants would slow him down should his intentions prove anything other than genuine.

As we walked towards the strawberry patch, we made small talk. It was strange that we had never met. His own family's farm was about ten miles from mine as the crows fly. I'd passed it a thousand times and watched the cows grow year after year, but never knew who ran it. We knew all of the same people in town, all of the same hiking and hunting spots, and I was even friends with a few of his old schoolmates. I felt silly for questioning if I was safe with him.

After we had filled his basket, I gave him a little tour of the farm. I felt at ease as I explained what I was doing and how I had made changes since my grandparents' passing. We exchanged stories and laughed. He had a deep, bellowing laugh. It was nearing lunchtime when we ended the tour back at his truck. He pulled a handful of neatly folded bills from his back pocket and handed them to me. I gently pushed his hand back.

"Consider it a birthday present," I said.

He smiled. "Well, thank you. Then would you let me use it to take you to dinner?"

I felt my heart do a summersault. I hadn't been on a date in... well... it had been a minute. I looked up into those soft, blue eyes and smiled.

"I think that'd be alright."

He excitedly opened the truck. He set the basket in the passenger seat and re-emerged with a pencil and a receipt.

"Your phone number?" he asked as he handed them to me.

I was a little caught off guard. It had been years since someone had asked me to handwrite a phone number. Most people just plugged it into their cellphones or I handed them a business card and that was that. I shrugged my shoulders and complied. He thanked me again and I watched the cloud of dust roll back down my driveway.

The rest of the day was a blur. I was walking on air as I completed my tasks for the day. Having spent so much time with Josh that morning had completely demolished my schedule and I ended up not finishing until after dark. But I didn't mind.

He called me that night. In fact, he called me every night right up until our date the following Friday. The quaint, family-owned restaurant was packed but we only saw each other. I told him about the tumultuous relationship with my brother, my parents back in West Virginia, and how I hoped I was making my grandparents proud by continuing on with the farm. In turn, he told me about how he was the youngest of four. He was his mother's favorite but he never really had a good relationship with his dad. He was married right out of high school but divorced by twenty-five. He said he refused to let it make him bitter. Young and dumb was nothing to be bitter about.

As we ate, we laid out our entire pasts for the other to see. It was pure honesty; almost as if we were seeing what it would take to scare the other one off. But we both stayed. At the end of the night, he walked me back to my truck. He wrapped his arms around me. Getting lost in his bulk and muscle brought new meaning to the term 'bear hug.' He held open my truck door for me and held my hand like a gentleman as I climbed in.

"Can we maybe do this again sometime?" he asked.

I closed the truck door and leaned out the open window. "I like Italian. Find somewhere with good meatballs and you got yourself a deal."

"You got it!" He was beaming as I backed the truck out of the parking spot.

I hardly slept that night. I was completely cloud-worthy. The next night, we resumed our regular phone calls. It was the thing I looked forward to most of all every day. The weekend after our date, he took me out to probably the fanciest restaurant I had ever been to. I felt so out of place in my skirt and frilly tank top. In contrast, he in his short-sleeved button-down shirt and faded red ball cap didn't seem to notice all of the sideways glances that were directed toward us. For our third date, he came to my house for a home-cooked meal and sat around a fire and watched the lightning bugs. He didn't leave until the next morning.

That was it. For the next three years, we were each other's entire world. We helped on each other's farms and attended holidays and family gatherings together. He even helped me bury my favorite barn cat on the North side of the strawberry patch where I was sure we wouldn't disturb any other remains. He was protective, almost to a fault. He often worried that I would get hurt in a field by myself and he didn't trust the hogs. His watchful nature was the source of virtually all of the only arguments we ever had. We shared a bed several nights a week and more in the cold winters. It was a happiness I had never known I was missing.

I had dated enough men to count on my fingers and toes throughout the entirety of my life. Never before had I felt like one could make me utter the words "'til death do us part.' On September eighteenth, when I was thirty-two, he presented me with a ring and I agreed that in a year's time, I would say those words to him.

A year was not enough. The following nine months were a whirlwind. His sister wanted to host a bridal shower for me and my mother wanted to take me dress shopping. She also wanted to hire another PI to find my brother and invite him to the wedding, but I told her not to bother. Even if I thought he would show up, he wasn't welcome. This made her cry, which made my father angry. It took a great deal of restraint to keep from lashing out and losing control of my temper. There were flowers, a caterer, and a church to coordinate as well. All of this was on top of my already busy farm life. It was almost too much. I was under a tremendous amount of pressure and finding it harder to keep it contained.

One evening, about two months from our wedding, I was sitting back on the old tack trunk and trying not to cry. Josh came in and found me. He pulled me to my feet and into him.

"Feeling emotional?" he asked.

I nodded into his chest.

"It's not going to be easy for you to let go of this place. I get that. But I'm here for you," he said.

I pushed back from him. "What do you mean 'let go?'" I asked.

He looked puzzled. "Isn't that why you're upset? Getting rid of the farm?"

I stared at him. "I'm overwhelmed from all of this wedding business. Why would I get rid of the farm?" I asked.

"We're getting married," he laughed. "We can't keep living in separate houses."

"I know that, but it still doesn't explain why I would need to sell this farm." I could feel my heart beating faster and my muscles begin to tingle.

"My farm is actually profitable. You barely make ends meet here. It makes more sense for you to focus on *our* farm."

I looked around the barn. I realized that in all the years of honest conversations we'd had together, this was never among them. By putting a ring on my finger, he expected me to sell my childhood, my inheritance, and my life's labor.

"I'm not selling this farm," I stated as I felt my cheeks get hot.

"Well, you can't keep it," he challenged.

"Watch me!" I almost yelled.

"I forbid it!" he blurted out.

"Forbid?!" I heard myself shriek the word.

Everything I had suppressed over the previous year came boiling to the surface despite my best efforts to restrain it. I could no longer hold back the tears of raw emotion and they came streaming down my face.

His anger started to match my own. "I'm not going to keep letting you be out here by yourself day after day until something bad happens to you. This argument is ridiculous. Now, we're getting married and you're selling this farm!"

"Wrong on both!" I ripped the ring off my finger and threw it at his feet.

"Andi! Now don't be unreasonable!"

I heard my brother's voice leave his lips. More than ten years before, those same words had been spoken in that same tack room over the same dispute. My vision went white with rage. I grabbed the steel scoop shovel that was leaning against the stall door. Before he could react, I brought it across his temple. I was small, but decades of hard labor had left me strong for my size. He stumbled. This time, I didn't stop after one blow. He fell to his knees after the second. I kept hitting him even after he was lying motionless on the ground. I kept swinging until I could no longer lift my arms.

There was a flutter in the hay loft. In that moment, I knew this time there had been a witness. The pale, moon face of the owl looked down at me. I looked out the barn door and into the starry night. She should have still been hunting, but instead, she had returned early to behold what I had done.

Feeling physically, mentally, and emotionally exhausted, I hitched one of his legs each to Max and Noah. They dragged him out to the South side of the strawberry patch. I carefully peeled up the top layer of soil that was knitted together by the roots of the plants. It was difficult, but it came up like a carpet. I had done this many times and I had developed a tried-and-true technique for it. The soil underneath was mixed with hard Ohio clay. I drove my Bobcat out to the patch and used the backhoe to dig the grave. As I moved the earth, I saw a brown orb surface. I jumped down to get a better look. I pulled it from the soil. My brother's eyeless orbits looked back at me. On the side was a crack from where that same shovel had hit him more than a decade before. He had taken quite some time to die that night while I had dug his resting place. He was never missed.

I had hoped he would have been more decayed, but I put the skull back and continued digging. After several hours, Josh was laid to rest. I put the plants over his grave, confident that next year's crop would be beautiful. In a few days, after a good rain helped the soil settle, I would file a missing person report and frantically call his family a mess with worry.

Tears returned and flowed over my cheeks. Despite this argument and that we had seen such different futures together, I truly did love him. But despite my love for him, my love for the life I had built was far greater. It was a life I would give everything, including him, to protect.

I glanced back at the barn. The owl watched me through the loft window. She was my only witness, and she would never tell.

5

What Needed to be Done

They promised the machines would make life better. They promised the people would have more leisure time and a family life. They lied. What started with automated computer and car factories with only skeleton crews to man them expanded. The first indication that there was a problem came in 2023 with the first fully-automated fast food restaurant. 3.1 million fast food workers in the United States quickly found themselves replaced by robotics. One person manned each restaurant- an armed security guard to prevent theft of food and cash.

Soon after, baristas at chain coffee shops were muscled out by bots that could work faster, didn't need to be paid, and could produce a more consistent product from store to store. Next came the delivery drones. Why pay drivers to tour all around town and waste expensive gasoline when a robot could load product onto an electric drone with the delivery address preprogrammed? Your order could be at your door in as soon as a few hours. Check-out clerks were replaced with self-scanners. That was if you shopped in the store. Most people shopped online and had a drone deliver their groceries for the week.

Not even higher-skilled jobs were safe. Telemedicine was replaced with artificial intelligence. Have a video chat with an AI and facial recognition could identify your rash, mucus, or whatever else ailed you and have a drone with appropriate medication at your door by the end of the next business day as long as you could pay.

Pay. There was the problem. Without payroll costs, most businesses' profits boomed. They did not pass those savings on to the consumers. Corporate greed prevailed. Now, not only were the people who relied on subordinate labor positions out of work, they had no way to afford basic essentials. Federal unemployment payments and assistance programs were chipped away little by little. Those who were lucky enough to have a college education in fields that hadn't been replaced were not much better off. Paying jobs didn't pay well and higher education came with a lifetime of debt. In 2023, nearly a quarter of Americans in their thirties lived with their parents. Most of the rest lived with roommates or significant others. By 2050, 82% still lived with their parents.

The 2040s saw a mass American exodus as people fled to Europe in hopes of a better life. Nearly twenty percent of adults tried to escape across the ocean where things were a little better, not much, but better. This became a blessing in disguise to millions as abandoned houses and businesses gave haven to the homeless, also known as fourth-class citizens.

Now, it is April of 2056. My name is Nevaeh. I am riding my bike home. It is rainy and the cold puddles splash at my legs. I feel chilled to my very core. It is hard to steer over my full backpack. Stuffed with what groceries I could manage to get this week, I ride with it at my front in an attempt to keep the precious cargo as dry as possible. I have a good haul. I managed to get enough synthetic meat that we can have two meals out of it this week.

I turn right onto a street of hundred-year-old prefabricated houses from the 1950s. Many are losing their siding and are wrapped in tarps or other scavenged plastics. Those that don't are rental properties that are in slightly better shape only because the law requires it. Our house is mostly intact. It has all of the windows and only a small section is protected with a tarp. It is less than one thousand square feet but, despite being small, it has three bedrooms. I am one of the lucky ones. I legally own my home. Nowadays, that is virtually unheard of. In the 2020s, the government allowed corporations to purchase properties for pennies on the dollar and rent them back to people at absurdly high rates. My mother, seeing what was going on, refused to sell her hard-earned home despite a multitude of offers. When she was killed a few years ago for the contents of her purse, the house and its remaining payments became mine.

I ride my bicycle up the crumbling driveway and enter through the back door, directly into the kitchen. I shake the water off and look to the living room as I set the heavy bag of food on the floor and work my soggy shoes off my feet.

Ayden, my life partner, is sitting on the couch. He is listening to music on the radio, the only free media entertainment left, and drawing. I smile. The images he makes with such simple tools as crayons and paper are stunning and creating them brings him such joy, but the world will never see them.

He looks up at me and smiles.

"You look like a drowned cat," he says.

"Next time it rains, you can get the groceries," I retort.

He stands, puts his hands on my shoulders, and kisses my forehead. I instantly feel the chill in my bones lift.

"Why don't you go get changed into something warm and dry while I put the groceries away," he offers.

I nod. This is not an argument. I am cold and tired. I stomp down the hall towards our bedroom. To the right, I pass the chicken room. I look in through the screen door. All nine hens and one rooster are scratching at the wood chips on the floor. I would much rather have them outside in their pen where they belong. In the summer we put them out for fresh air and sunlight when we can be with them to guard them. Predators are not a problem since the local government had most of the coyote population exterminated more than a decade ago. My flock is valuable and neighbors will not hesitate to steal them. A single chicken may feed you for a day or two but my girls are good layers and their eggs are our primary protein source. I let them hatch a few clutches a year and sell the chicks to make ends meet. I will not overbreed them. It reduces the quality of their eggs to let them have too many clutches and I must feed my family first. Several of the girls look up at me and the rooster fluffs his feathers in threat. Despite the food, warmth, and safety I provide him, he is eternally ungrateful. I appreciate the fact that he produces such good chicks. That and the fact that I can no longer smell him.

At the end of the hall, the door to the right leads to Ayden's brother Jaxson's room. He shares the space with his partner, Emmalee. They help relieve the burden of living expenses so despite the fact that I do not like either of them as people, their presence is welcome. Jaxson works night security at the grocery store so he is asleep. Emmalee usually works around four in the evening to four in the morning. She is a waitress in the high-roller room at the casino. Men with money still prefer their cocktails served with a smile in a short skirt. Even though she only makes three dollars an hour, what she brings home in tips often makes me wish I too had boobs and lighter hair.

I turn left into the room I share with Ayden. It's small. There is only enough space for our bed, two bedside tables, and a dresser. The closet door hangs open and Ayden's dirty clothes lie on the floor next to the hamper. There is a tiny house spider in the corner watching over our little corner of the world. The bed remains unmade and a basket of clean laundry lays at its foot. I sigh.

I find clean pair of pants and a t-shirt in the broken plastic basket. I shed my wet clothes and go to bathroom across from the chickens. I turn on the shower and step into the tub. The water is hot, steamy, and comforting. I feel the warmth move into my body and I begin to thaw. I would love to stay in here but clean, potable water is scarce and expensive. I stay just long enough to regain feeling in my nose and toes. I rub the sliver of soap over myself, rinse, and exit the tub. As I towel my body, the smell of hot soup drifts down the hall from the kitchen. My stomach roars in indignation at my failure to realize it is empty.

Dressed, I make my way to the kitchen. I take my seat at the table as Ayden sets a steaming bowl in front of me. I cup my hands around the bowl allowing the heat to move into my fingers. He sits to my right and smiles at me.

"You survived another day at work," he says both as a statement and a question.

I work at a state-funded daycare that provides services to people in similar financial situations to my own. Children are expensive and good daycare is around twenty-five hundred dollars a month. Regular people like myself cannot afford it and because our parents cannot afford to retire, there is rarely family to relieve the burden. The children I work with are generally accidents that families cannot afford. Class one and two citizens who can afford children but can't have them would rather undergo fertility treatments, in vitro, or surrogate just to have a child with their genetic makeup so those that may have been adoptable are not. This is where facilities like mine come in. We make sure the kids are provided at least one meal per day. We have creams and ointments for rashes and sometimes bathe the children if it is clear they have no running water at home. It is exhausting and sometimes heartbreaking work, but I love what I do and I love those kids.

I sigh. "For now," I answer him. "They are talking about cutting funding again."

He shakes his head and looks down at his soup.

"What were you drawing when I came in?" I ask, eager to change the subject.

He smiles and finishes chewing the vegetables in his mouth.

"The dog I saw today," he says brightly.

"What kind of dog?"

"Big black thing. I was stocking the drink machine at All-Mart and a guy had him on a bright red leash. Beautiful! And so friendly!" His smile faded. "I hope we can get a dog someday."

I choke on my soup a little. "I know, Honey, but it's so hard to afford a dog. One bag of food is over a hundred dollars. Never mind the licensing fees and taking it to the vet. I don't know if we'll ever be able to afford one."

"I know," he looks sullen. "Maybe I can teach the rooster to play fetch."

I smile at his attempt to cheer himself up. We finish our meal with a conversation about our day and sit on the couch together listening to the radio for an hour before he retires to bed. I stay up a little longer. I am reading a novel on my tablet about a woman who can speak to a demon that helps bring revenge on those who wrong her. I love books. By choosing a book, I get to choose a different reality – a different existence – than the one I have. I know my life could be much harder but I read books from the nineteen-nineties and two-thousands, before robots and artificial intelligence, and I think of how much better life was when people could afford to live and everyone had cars and food. They took it all for granted.

I hear a door at the end of the hall open and close. Jaxson shuffles toward me in his boxer shorts. It is ten-thirty and his day is just beginning. He stops and yawns. He scratches the back of his head, further ruffling his already shaggy brown hair.

"Hi," he yawns again as he speaks and changes to scratching his bare chest. "Is there food?"

I nod. "There is leftover soup in the fridge," I say. "The yard will need to be cut when you get home so we don't get fined."

Our lawn bot is so old it doesn't know the day of the week anymore so it can't be programmed to run on a schedule. It also likes to wander off so if you don't keep an eye on it, it could end up a few houses away before you notice there's a problem.

He nods and turns into the bathroom, closing the door behind him. Upon hearing the percussion of flatulence he produces, I decide to go to bed. I close the door behind me softly. Ayden is snoring loudly as I crawl under the covers and pull a pillow over my head to muffle the sound.

It is Monday morning. The *beep beep beep* of the alarm jolts me awake. The bed is empty. Ayden left hours ago to start his day. I turn off the alarm and stretch as I lay on my back. I feel the satisfying clicks and cracks of my joints as they snap into place. I dress and make my way to the kitchen. I can hear the television from Jaxson and Emmalee's room. She arrived home barely an hour ago and was likely eating in their room. She and I hardly interact. She prefers to spend her alone time in their room, watching the TV. Her tips are enough that they can pay for two streaming services per month. Sometimes, I can hear them laughing at something and would like to watch it too, but it is theirs that they pay for and it doesn't feel right to try to make them share. Besides, Ayden has his art, I have my library books, and we all have the radio.

On the kitchen table there is a receipt for a funds transfer. Emmalee has paid her share of the bills into the joint account.

Next to the receipt sits three eggs. The girls have had a good morning and Ayden has left me what he didn't eat. I fry my eggs, drink some orange juice, and set off to work.

The sun is just trying to come up and the sky is changing from purple to pink. The air is moist and the ground is still wet from yesterday's rain. A block from work, an ADV (Automated Delivery Vehicle) speeds past me in the motorized vehicle lane. It splashes the left side of my body, the cold water soaking my coat. I swear at it and display a hand gesture that the driver of a car believes is for him. He returns in kind.

The building I work in is large. The top floors are office spaces for various mid-level businesses, the middle floor has several studios for dance and yoga instruction, and the ground level is leased space for people trying to make a living. In addition to our childcare center, there is a jewelry store, a furniture consignment, a bakery, and a clothing reseller among other businesses managing to hang on.

I ride my bike straight up to the back door. I use my ID to open the door and roll my bike in with me. Technically, employee bicycle parking is in the underground garage. The building owners do not like the unseemly display of bicycles, indicating that there are people in the building who are poor and therefore giving the building a bad image. Most of us *are* poor; I don't know who they think they are fooling. They said the underground garage is to keep our bikes dry and safe but we know better. The nicer businesses on the top two floors have an image to maintain which is why they have a private lobby with an elevator that we are not allowed access to. We undesirables could hurt business. Their lobby has its own security team while no one watches the garage. Bike theft and armed robbery are a constant concern and one of the yoga instructors was abducted by her estranged husband down there. This is why I hide my bike in the furnace room, chain it to a pipe, and put the handlebars in my bookbag for good measure.

I am fifteen minutes early to the childcare center. It operates twenty-four hours a day as many of the parents have two or even three jobs. One little boy stayed with us for four days straight when his mother, having worked over forty hours without rest, collapsed from exhaustion. It was over a day later when a family member came to retrieve him.

I shed my coat and hang it on the peg in our little office space. I am grateful that, though it is soaked, my sweater is mostly dry.

"You look rough," I hear my friend and colleague, Addyson say.

I turn to her. She is the picture of a morning person. Her brown hair is neat and pulled high in a ponytail. Her big opal eyes are bright and ready to start the day. Her bright yellow sweatshirt and beaming personality make her the personification of sunshine. She is my friend and I love her, but this early in the morning, I hate her.

"Come on," she says. "Let's get some coffee before the shift starts. My treat."

I look behind her at the queue of first shift children being dropped off as the third shift children are awakened grumpily to go home. She doesn't have to ask me twice and we go to the coffee shop on the other end of the first floor.

Real coffee is expensive and I hate to spend my friend's

money frivolously. I step up to the barista bot. The AI has been given a humanoid form with long blonde hair and eyes that are completely dead. I order roasted dandelion root tea, which tastes very similar to real coffee, with a shot of caffeine powder and vanilla milk. Addyson orders caffeinated chicory with sugar.

"Would you like a donut?" the bot asks.

"No, thank you," Addyson answers and inserts her credit card.

The machine behind the counter whirrs to life making our drinks.

"Thank you and have a wonderful day!" the barista-bot says.

We step to the side to allow the person behind us to order. Our drinks come down the conveyer belt and onto the rollers where we retrieve them.

I hold the waxed paper cup to my lips and inhale deeply through my nostrils. It isn't real coffee, but it is caffeinated, slightly bitter, and hot. I take a big gulp and allow it to lightly scald my throat.

We walk past the bakery where, through the window, we can see kneading machines working some kind of bread dough, a decorating machine piping precisely calculated colored icing on a personalized cake, and an attendant organizing orders as they roll out of various ovens. I wonder how such a small operation stays in business. Most bakeries have dozens of these machines and can fulfill hundreds of orders per day of everything from ornate wedding cakes to soft pretzels, to specialty breads and even pastries.

The clothing reseller is straightening a sweatshirt on a mannequin in the front window. I think of how much Ayden would probably like it but looks like it would be too small from this far away. I make a mental note to stop by after my shift to check. It's never too early to start thinking about birthday presents.

We return to the childcare center and clock in two minutes early. I finish my dandelion root and listen to rounds from the third shift about who is staying into our shift, that the automated vacuum is on strike after sucking up some small game pieces, and that management put word out that they will be by sometime soon for observations. Great.

Addyson and I thank them and send them on their way. We turn and face the children. Around forty sleepy but eager bodies ranging in age from a few weeks to five years are strewn around the room.

"Who wants story time?" Addyson calls.

Around half of the children yell with excitement and run to the story corner. She loads a book into the old robot that was an adult human-sized teddy bear. He comes to life and greets the kids. They wave back. He begins to tell the story as images of his narration show on the screen on the bookshelf behind him.

I begin moving the youngest children to the nursery area. Ten cribs line the walls opposite each other. These spaces are for the littlest ones who cannot quite stand yet. I prefer the nursery. When I was a little girl, I dreamed of having a baby. My favorite doll's name was Angel. She had curly hair and round lips like mine. But, as with most childhood dreams, it was murdered at the onset of adulthood. There came the realization that motherhood is a lifelong expense that I can never afford. At work, at least, I get to cuddle them, care for them, educate them, and watch the grow before they venture on to grade school. For many of these children, the care that Addyson and I provide is the closest thing to affection they receive. Busy parents living in what essentially amounts to poverty do not have time for children they didn't want and cannot afford.

Not that I want to play favorites, but I am particularly fond of Fang. I don't know who he belongs to. A slew of people have dropped him off or picked him up, all claiming to be aunts and uncles or cousins. They always come with his key card- the plastic card with his information and password- so we release him to these strangers. As a state-operated facility, we are not supposed to ask too many questions. I have hated the few times he has left on my shift. No one seems happy to see him. His retrieval is a chore they would rather not do. Twice he has cried when he left me. Part of me wants to cry too and I wonder if they would even care if I took him home with me.

I don't know what makes Fang so special. He was one of the smallest babies I've ever worked with. He only weighed a little under five pounds when he started coming to our facility at two weeks old. Every day for two years I have cleaned him, fed him, hugged him, and put brightly colored adhesive bandages on his booboos. I am uniquely attached to him and he is to me. I can't bear the thought of how I will manage to cope when it is his turn to move on.

I get the eight littlest children cleaned up and placed in their cribs. As I expected, they all had dirty diapers and empty tummies. I program the food dispenser to make nine hundred and fifty milliliters of formula to be placed in bottles.

Further down the line, Addyson has managed to wrangle five toddlers, clean them, and place them in a containment pen with toys and snacks. Fang comes to the edge of the pen as I walk by and I give him a hug. The story ends and the older children start to get up, some complaining they are hungry, and some pulling out toys. Addyson helps me dispense the bottles to the infants by programming the robotic arms that would keep the bottle presented to the baby and monitor how much they eat by the change in weight of the bottles. We will return to burp them in a moment. We turn on the television and start passing out bowls of dry cereal to the hungry older children.

This is how we spend our day. We move as an efficient team between the infants and older children. We change diapers, help with potty training, break up fights, provide education and entertainment, feed, wash, and repeat. We fix the robot vacuum and it works on overdrive cleaning up the floors. If it becomes sentient, it will resign. We sneak bites of food for ourselves where we can and when we can.

At two in the afternoon, Colton, the man from the laundry service, comes for our dirty crib linens, rags, towels, and assorted other items while he drops off the crisp, clean ones. I smile as I watch Addyson try to contain her flirting. They are around the same age, nearly ten years my junior. He is tall with neatly cut brown hair and brown eyes. While he's not my type, I can see the appeal. Addyson, like all people in their early twenties, lives with her parents so they can share the bills. I've never known her to date and never heard her mention a boyfriend, but her eyes light up when Colton comes twice a week. Unfortunately, I don't think she will give him a real chance at love. She has mentioned too many times that she doesn't think real love is something she can feel. I never understand what she means by that.

At four o'clock, the next shift arrives and we do our rounds. Addyson and I say goodbye and she heads off to her car in the garage while I get my bike. I step out into the bright pre-evening sunlight. It is unfortunately deceptively chilly despite the sun, but the beauty of the day is not lost on me as I mount my bike and begin to cut through the parking lot. A Mercedes almost hits me and sends me to the pavement. The owner of the vehicle doesn't even look up from his phone as the AutoDrive continues to chauffeur him to his destination. I curse and look at the rip in my pants. It will need to be patched.

I go home for dinner with Ayden, read, and sleep. The next day I do it again. And the next day. And the next. On the weekend, I clean, muck the chickens, and tend to the garden while Ayden is at his second job. He works for a small phone repair company shipping questionably fixed electronics back to their owners. It is under the table at a cash-only business. It isn't ideal, but it helps with the bills. I had had a weekend job stocking garment racks at All-Mart but lost the position when they brought in the AI-equipped stocking robots.

On Sunday, a truck rolls into my front yard. Jaxson and Emmalee open the front door and start carrying boxes out to the truck.

"What's going on?" I ask.

"All-Mart has offered me an apartment in employee housing. Me and Emmalee want to have our own space," Jaxson answers.

"Why haven't you said something sooner?" I demand answers.

"We didn't know how to break it to you." Emmalee comes up behind Jaxson and puts a reassuring hand on his shoulder. "So, we didn't."

"So, your cowardice leaves Ayden and me no time to prepare?"

I am fuming. I feel my face getting hot and I am trying not to yell.

"Call it what you want," she says. "This is a good thing. You should be happy for us."

"Ha!" I screech and throw the nearest thing to me, a pillow off the couch, directly at her face.

She ducks and shrugs her shoulders.

"Come on Jax, let's load up."

They must have been packing through the week while Ayden and I were at work. All of their things had been neatly boxed and with the help of Emmalee's brother who had driven the truck and two moving robots to do the heavier lifting, they have their room cleared out in less than an hour. I do not say goodbye or wave as they drive off to their new lives.

I am standing in the doorway of their room, wondering what we are going to do when Ayden comes home. I explain what happened. Angry, he repeatedly tries to call his brother but his calls go unanswered. Jaxson and Ayden were close only out of necessity but I never saw him doing this. Emmalee doesn't really seem to care for anyone but hadn't I given her a place in my home? Done her grocery shopping? Kept her living space clean? This betrayal goes far deeper than money.

The next morning, I vent my frustration to Addyson over

dandelion root tea, her treat again. She doesn't seem to understand where I am coming from but lends a sympathetic ear.

A month goes by. Ayden and I work hard to cover the slack in chores. Because I only work one job, I take on the brunt of the extra duties. It is a fact that I try hard not to resent Ayden for but I hear the strain in my voice when we talk. We bicker over little things that never used to be a problem before and I feel a new distance between us. All the extra work at home makes finding time to look for a second job difficult but still, I try. Without it, we make ends meet but only just. What little we used to put away into savings will now have to cover the bills that Jaxson and Emmalee so callously left us with. I interview for dozens of positions without success. Very few positions require human labor. Those subordinate labor positions that are available are competitive and often dangerous. But I must try. I must.

Every day I go to work at the childcare facility. It keeps me busy and my mind from focusing on my fear of the future. Little Fang comes to me for hugs and to show me pictures he has colored during art time. I feel the little hole in my heart plug temporarily every time he comes to me.

It is nearly June. The summer heat is already bearing down. I can feel it radiating from the pavement as I pedal home. I am worried. I tried to pay for groceries but my card was declined. That has never happened. Has my identity been stolen? Did Ayden buy something without telling me? We've been strained lately but that is not something he would do.

As I turn onto my street, I see a police vehicle in my driveway. This is not good.

A bespeckled officer in a crisp black uniform and shiny gold badge steps out of the vehicle.

"Are you Nevaeh Carter?" he asks me.

"Yes," I answer.

I can't hear myself speak. All I hear is the pounding of my heart in my ears.

"Do you know a..." he flips his notebook. "Ayden Poole?"

"Yes. He is my S.O."

"Shortly after o-seven hundred hours this morning Mr. Poole was shot in a robbery in which the perpetrators made off with his truck of food for stocking the dispensers. The GPS on the truck has been disabled. Are you aware of anyone who was following Mr. Poole or that he may have shared his route with?"

"Shot?!" I gasp. I think my heart stops. "Where is he? Is he okay?"

"My most recent information is that Mr. Poole is alive in University Hospital. Ma'am, I need you to focus and answer my questions so we can locate the stolen vehicle."

"The truck? What about the person who shot Ayden?"

"If we can locate the thief, he will be brought to justice."

Thief? Of course, they are worried about the truck. Ayden's employer will value profit over life every time. It doesn't matter that they can write the truck and merchandise off as a loss when stolen. As long as it is missing, it hurts productivity. Ayden is replaceable.

Frustrated and scared, I answer the rest of the officer's questions so that I can go to Ayden as quickly as possible. When the officer finally finishes his inane line of questioning, I get a running start on my bike and pedal as hard and as fast as I can. University hospital is around twelve miles from my house and if I ride hard, I can be there in an hour.

What if the cop is wrong? What if Ayden has already died? We've not been fighting but things between us have been tense. What if we aren't able to make amends? He is my other half. I don't want to live without him and I can't bear the idea that he has died believing I am angry with him or blame him in any way for the situation we are in.

When I arrive at the hospital, I chain my bike to the bike rack and put the handlebars in my backpack. I take my identification, wallet, and phone out of the bag before placing it on the security scanner. I hand my ID card to a security guard before entering the body scanner. My bag is confiscated as I expected it to be. I then get in line for the information kiosks. I bounce. I tap my foot. I try not to scream as I feel like I am crawling out of my skin. This is agony.

It is finally my turn. I insert my ID card into the kiosk and scan my finger. Finally, it offers to assist me. I type in Ayden's information. As his recognized emergency contact, it permits me the information. He is in room four thirty-two, suite A. He had surgery and is able to accept visitors. A map of his location appears on the screen. I request a guide and a little red drone carried by four propellers pops out of the top of the kiosk. The little screen on the bottom displays Ayden's name as it buzzes down the hallway with me in pursuit.

We get on the elevator with several other people and a few other guide drones. On the fourth floor, we exit and I am led through a maze of dimly lit halls. I am just thinking of how glad I am that I didn't try to find his room on my own when the drone suddenly stops. Its little screen flashes *'have a nice day'* before it zips back down the hall. I look at the room to my right. Ayden is sleeping. I approach him quietly, unsure if I may wake him. He is pale but alive. His personal effects lay on the table beside him. I touch the screen on the tablet next to him and turn it on. I tap "Update Family" and the screen changes.

Ayden Poole. Thirty-Three-year-old male. Class 3 citizen. Uninsured. Unemployed. Gunshot wound. Bullet entered caudal and lateral to left clavicle. Exited medial to left scapula. Negligible damage to scapular bone. Transfused two pints type O Faux-Globin. Wounds sealed with elastic protein and grafting mesh. To be released upon settlement of payment.

He is okay. He is going to be okay. I breathe heavily with relief and feel tears burn my eyes. I re-read the report two more times before I see it. Unemployed. I begin to shake. I take his ID from his wallet on the table and tap it on the tablet.

Ayden Neo Poole. Class 3 citizen. Male. DOB: November 1st, 2022. Eyes brown. Hair brown. Address: 8018 Sanctuary Road. Emergency Contact: Nevaeh Olivia Carter. Vehicle license: motorized. 244 transit points available. Last known Employment: Turner Foods. Terminated due to failure to protect stock and dereliction of duties. Credit score: 438. Assets frozen due to outstanding medical debt.

I stop reading. Assets frozen. That is why I could not use our joint card to buy food.

I navigate back to the main screen on the tablet. I tap "view bill." $38,258.72 appears on the screen and the numbers steadily climb as hospitalization is charged per minute. I panic. I feel sick. What are we going to do? We can't pay this. Gently shake Ayden awake.

"Honey?' I ask.

He groans but opens his eyes.

"Honey, how do you feel? We need to get you out of here," I say as I try to contain the urgency in my voice.

His left arm is bound in a sling so he pushes himself up with his right.

"What's going on?" he asks.

"You were shot at work. They took the food and your truck. You're in the hospital. Your bill is forty thousand and the longer you stay, the higher it will get. Are you well enough to come home?"

His eye bulge and all grogginess seems to instantly leave him. He tries to push himself out of the bed.

I tap the checkout button on the tablet. It asks how we would like to pay. Under "Payment Plans" it says the option is not available due to unemployment. I look up at Ayden as he tries to dress himself with only one arm. How are we going to do this? I put in my information as the payer. The only payment option that becomes available is "Dock Pay" but the option comes with a 24% interest cost. I swallow hard as I sign the agreement with my finger.

Ayden takes the bus home while I ride my bike. It was hard enough when I was looking for a second job but now my pay will be docked and he has no fulltime employment. At least there is still some money coming in from the electronics repair. It isn't much and cannot be legally reported, but it's something. Once home and Ayden is settled in, I cry myself to sleep.

For the next week, I dutifully go to work while Ayden applies to every job opening he sees. My first docked paycheck is painful to look at and I stare out into my yard and wonder if the grass is edible. We will not be able to continue without another income for long. We have some savings to pull us through, but not much.

The following Monday there is chaos at the childcare center as a woman I have never seen before is attempting to do both intake and release in the morning rush. I look over at the glass window of our office. A woman in a suit is talking to the two third shift girls. They both look like they may cry.

I look in the other direction and against the wall I see a person – no, not a person – sitting in a big red chair. I cautiously walk up to it.

It is a robot made to look male. It has been given bright blue eyes and blonde hair. It blinks and looks at me.

"Good morning, Nevaeh," it says.

I jump back and stifle a scream. The storytime bear had certainly never called me by name. What is this thing?

"What is it?" Addyson comes to stand next to me.

"Good morning, Addyson. My name is Zacc. Nice to meet you," it says to her.

"Isn't he beautiful!" An unfamiliar voice sings out from behind us.

The woman in the suit comes up to us with her arms spread. Behind her, I see the third shift girls getting their things silently, still looking like they may cry. Aren't we going to do rounds?

The woman in the suit continues. "I'm Jennifer Connell. I'm this branch's corporate liaison."

I feel instantly uneasy.

"This is the Zenith Automated Child Care system. Isn't he great!" Jennifer exclaims.

"What does he do?" Addyson asks warily.

"Everything! He is hard-wired into the building so he can play movies, games, or read stories. He can control the TV. He can give out snacks." She gestures to a new station against the wall that looks like a row of small silos with dispensing funnels at the top. "He has the latest facial recognition software to be able to identify the individual kids. He can also analyze their expressions to determine what emotion they are exhibiting and, with his thirty-eight cameras all around the center and AI that can identify potentially dangerous behaviors, he'll never miss a thing! You won't even have to do rounds with the shifts before or after you because Zacc here will track everything!"

I find her excitement disturbing. I'm right.

"For the next thirty days, he'll be working alongside you and getting to know the routine here and analyzing your work. At the end of the thirty days, he will make a determination on which person from each shift he will be replacing."

"What?!" Addyson and I exclaim in unison.

"You can't really expect one person to oversee forty children alone," I say.

"It won't be one person. It will be one of you and Zacc. Do you have thirty-eight eyes watching every corner of this facility? Because he does. Your role will be to complete the duties he can't including changing diapers, putting them down for naps, etc. His job is to provide the enrichment and nutrition.'

"Children need more than enrichment and nutrition. They

need affection and nurturing," I glance over at Fang as I continue my protest.

"It is not this facility's job to provide affection. That's why they have families. This is a state-funded facility. Our job is to keep them alive so their parents can be productive members of society until they are old enough to go to school and learn how to be productive members of society themselves. We didn't take the decision lightly. We even opted for a male automated system to ensure the children have a male figure in their lives." Jennifer pats Zacc on the shoulder and it smiles.

"But—" I begin.

"Ladies, trust me. We have run numerous simulations and projections to assure us this is both beneficial for you and cost-cutting for us. We even pushed back his installation by over a month so we could put him to use on test groups to evaluate his efficacy. Now, I have to be off," Jennifer looks at her phone. "Good luck to both of you and have a great day!"

My heart sinks into my stomach and I feel sick. I look over at Addyson and she is shaking her head and staring at the robot. I look at it too. Despite being programmed to blink every six seconds like an average human, its eyes are cold and upsetting. Its latex face mimics human expressions accurately, but they aren't as realistic as the creator had intended. This *thing* is meant to replace one of us. Us. We don't just change diapers. We give hugs. We kiss booboos. We comfort them when they are scared. We model appropriate responses to emotions.

"Okay kids, gather around!" Zacc's sudden call to attention causes both Addyson and me to jump.

The children who can walk come over. Several hide behind

our legs. Fang reaches up for me and I set him on my hip. He hugs close into my side.

"My name is Zacc. I'm here to help all of you," the robot introduces itself. "Miss Addyson, Miss Nevaeh, and I are all here for you."

"I'm hungry." One of the nearly five-year-olds yells.

I look at the clock. By now we are usually providing breakfast and have most of the diapers changed.

"Okay, Robbie. Why doesn't everyone get some breakfast from the feeding station and I'll read you all a story while you eat." The robot gestures to the row of silos with its arm.

Several of the children cautiously approach the new apparatus. A blue plastic bowl pops out of a little window. None of the children touch it.

"It's okay," Zacc says. "New things are scary sometimes."

I look around at the hungry, scared faces. Most of them are looking to me and Addyson for guidance. I sigh. I weave my way through them and take the bowl. One of the silos lights up. I hold the bowl under it and cereal pours out. I hand the bowl to Robbie.

"Thank you," he says.

"Yes, thank you for demonstrating, Miss Nevaeh," the robot says.

I try to hide the look of disdain on my face as I take Fang with me to tend to the infants. Addyson looks far less concerned than I feel as she leads away two toddlers.

Over the following month, things go from bad to worse. Ayden cannot find work. His arm is in pain so severe that over-the-counter medicines don't touch it. He feels useless despite still working off the books on the weekends. He slips into a depression that I cannot bring him out of due to my own failing mental health. I watch our savings account shrink little by little. I decide to let our hens hatch a few clutches to sell the chicks but this decreases the eggs we have to eat. One of the hens becomes egg bound and dies before we can help her get the egg out. I cry as I prepare her for supper.

At work, things are not much better I will grudgingly admit that the robot's assistance does make some work lighter. We are still far too busy to believe that it could replace one of us. It can identify children fighting over a toy, but it cannot stop the fight or help the kids learn how to handle disputes. It cannot take potty-training toddlers to the restroom. It can hug children who are upset if they come to its chair, but they prefer to seek me out. And Fang, who always comes in a mess and craves affection, wants nothing to do with him. Sometimes I feel as though Addyson is being extra polite to the robot but decide it is my imagination.

At the end of the month, I say goodbye to Addyson and gather my things. As I walk past Zacc, it turns its dead, doll-like eyes to me.

"Have a great day, Nevaeh. It was nice working with you."

I stop. I turn to it.

"What did you say?" I ask it.

It blinks but does not answer.

I look around. The other shift has the children on the other side of the room to sing the birthday song to one of the toddlers.

"You're going to recommend me for termination, aren't you." I make this a statement, not a question.

"I am," it says simply.

"Why?" I ask.

"While you are clearly the more efficient worker and the children prefer you to Miss Addyson, I believe she would be a better choice."

"Why?" I repeat.

"Miss Addyson is more physically appealing which is a more comforting observation for parents."

"You're picking her because she is prettier?"

"Not only that. Her age is more conducive to this line of work. You are over thirty. Constantly lifting children causes wear on the human body. Miss Addyson will be able to fulfill her duties longer and more effectively. Also, I feel the hostility you feel towards me will interfere with our ability to work together as a cohesive team. Miss Addyson has demonstrated open friendliness and acceptance of me, which will put the children more at ease with my presence. It has been my observation that there is a mutual emotional attachment between you and many of these children and as long as that attachment to you is present and they see your hostility towards me, I will be unable to fulfill my role as child care provider."

"I'm being fired because I'm not pretty and the children love me too much."

"And because you hate me. I do not wish this to be personal but I cannot function to my full capacity as I was purchased to do as long as you are here.

Without control of my body, I lunge for it. It holds up its hands.

"I have thirty-eight cameras. If you break me, they will know."

I look over my shoulder at the children finishing the birthday treats the little girl's mother has brought. I can feel tears coming down my face as I rush from the center.

"Goodbye, Nevaeh," I hear it call after me.

As I pedal home, I find it hard to ride. I am shaking. My eyes are blurry with tears. What are we going to do? How are we going to live? When my unemployment is filed, they'll freeze our accounts again. I won't even be able to access what's left of our savings. I can't sell my mother's house; we'll have nowhere to live. We've both been trying to find work but we've both failed at every turn.

Then I think about Fang. He is the closest thing to a son I will ever have. I am supposed to have three more years with him before he moves on to grade school. Who is going to snuggle him and care for him for those three years? Certainly not those people who claim to be his family. And Addyson has never shown him any interest. What is he going to do without me? What am I going to do without him?

I lose myself in panic, but I do not know for how long. I suddenly realize I am nowhere near home. I am in a nice neighborhood with two-story houses with well-kept lawns. This is Addyson's neighborhood. I've been here once before when Adyen and I were invited to a barbeque.

I turn left towards a cul-de-sac and ride right up to her garage door. I try to pull myself together, climb the steps to her front door, and ring her doorbell.

She answers.

"Nevaeh! What are you doing here? Are you okay?"

I crumble there on her front porch. Tears pour from my eyes as I recount my conversation with the robot.

"Please," I beg her." "Please, you have to decline. You have to tell them I am the better choice."

"But you aren't the better choice," she says calmly. She kneels on the ground with me. "Zacc is right. You're too emotionally invested in those kids."

I feel tears subside as her words sink in. Hadn't she told me before that she can't feel love?

"You don't feel anything for them?" I ask.

My heart swells as I think of Fang.

"No," she almost laughs. "They aren't my kids. And besides, it's just a job."

"But it's a job I need. You don't. You live in this big house with your parents. You have help. Ayden and I have no one. I need this."

She shakes her head. "I'm sorry. I feel for you. I do. But I have a good life and I'm not going to throw that away for you."

"Please," I whisper.

"Sorry, Nevaeh." She helps me to my feet. "Maybe Ayden shouldn't have let all that food get stolen.'

I stare at her in disbelief. "Are you really blaming him for getting shot?"

She shrugs. "I'm just saying he worked a job that he knew was dangerous. And you knew you were going to have problems when his brother moved out. If you really wanted a second job, you could have had one by now. You guys' choices are the reasons you're in this position."

I am stunned but shock soon gives way to anger. How dare she? This spoiled idiot who has never known a struggle in her life has passed judgment on my existence?

"If you become a class four, let me know which soup kitchen you frequent and I'll make sure we bring something good for you at Christmas."

She says this with full sincerity. She is not mocking or being condescending. She truly believes that providing one meal a year is charity or doing her part.

"If I lose everything, it will be your fault and you think a can of soup at Christmas will make up for it?" I scream at her.

"My fault? Zacc chose me fair and square. You should have been nicer to him."

"It's a piece of equipment!"

"But he chose me."

"You don't even care about the job."

"No. But my apathy has allowed me to keep it. Your empathy will cost you everything."

I do not know if I hit her or if I shove her. I watch her go backwards over the edge of the porch. I hear her head thud against the edge of the bottom step. She is silent and her eyes are frozen in a permanent expression of disbelief as blood pools and stains the concrete walkway around her head.

I frantically look around but see no one. Most class two people are still at work this time of day. I look back at her. Do I leave her here? Do I hide her? No. I replay the last few minutes in my head. She felt nothing. Nothing for me, her work, or even the children. But without her, my job is secure. I can take care of Ayden and myself until we are back on our feet. I can be with Fang.

I look at the doorbell camera. They will know what happened. They will know it was me. But what would it show? Just an accident. Surely it will only show that she fell and hit her head. I call the emergency line and ask for an ambulance. I see the medics attempt to revive her while a cop asks me questions. Why was I, a class three citizen, in a class two neighborhood? How well did I know the victim? What were we arguing about? I begin to worry that he will not believe it is an accident as he continues his line of questioning for what feels like ages before he finally seems satisfied and I breathe. I see the coroner arrive and load the body onto a gurney. What I once saw as a friend, I now see for what she really was; a cold, unfeeling automaton. She was no more human than Zacc.

As I mount my bike and ride toward home, I realize that I have just taken a life. I should be distraught. But instead, I feel an unsettling sense of calm. I did what needed to be done to secure my family and for the first time in months, I am at peace.

6

To be a queen

    I dream a dream
To be a queen
And march ten thousand feet.
And if, by chance,
Quite happenstance,
A misogynist king I meet
I shall but show
My quiver and bow
And bring him to his knees.
All will know
Be friend or foe
A woman truly leads.

7

Tea

I was a shy girl growing up. The real world held very little interest to me. I preferred to hide in my room or under the tree in the backyard with a library book. As a child, I was bullied for my curly red hair and so only had a friend or two at a time. My true friends were my books. My adventures were within their pages and I frequently developed crushes on fictional characters. In high school, I had virtually no prospects for love or romance. I had a date here and there, but nothing profound. I was content with my life, though it was a slightly lonely one. Everything changed in my second year of college, and it all started with a cup of tea.

It was a cloudless late-summer day. I was leaning against the retaining wall on the campus quad, my head sticking out just above it. I was sitting cross-legged on the ground with a highlighter in my left hand, a hot cup of oolong with honey in my right, and a textbook in my lap. The air was warm, the sun was bright, and I found myself constantly distracted by campus goings-on. There were folding tables for the various groups and clubs to hand out fliers and ask for signatures on petitions. A group of ten or so joggers went by on the paved path. One of them stumbled and lost his rhythm when a pretty blonde girl waved at him which led to jeers and laughter from his friends. There were several couples sprawled out on the grass eating fast food and many other students who, like me, desperately needed to study but couldn't pass up such a beautiful day.

Somewhere in the distance, my distracted ears vaguely caught something to the effect of 'look out.' The next thing I knew, I felt something heavy hit the back of my head and I was forced to the ground. My hot tea splashed all over my arm and textbook.

When I stopped seeing stars, I pushed myself to my feet and surveyed the damage. My sweatshirt was soaked and my skin underneath was throbbing from the hot tea. My textbook had seen better days but would be salvageable. Then I looked up.

Standing in front of me was a man slightly taller than me holding a frisbee. He was wearing a white t-shirt and blue running shorts. His dark brown hair was neatly gelled in pace and his matching dark eyes displayed a look of utter horror. Despite his expression, I couldn't ignore how handsome he was.

"I'm so sorry! I-I didn't mean to," he sputtered. "Are you okay?"

I shook the remaining droplets of tea off of my hands and wiped them on my jeans.

"Yeah," I said with a note of disgruntlement. "What do you think you were doing?"

"I was chasing the frisbee." He held up the neon green disk. "I didn't see your head on the other side of the wall until it was too late. God, I'm so sorry."

"It's fine. It's fine," I said as I searched through the grass for my highlighter.

After I gathered my things, I stood and turned to face him. His expression had changed from horror to apology.

"My name's Luke." He held out this hand.

I hesitated but shook it. His hand was soft but strong. It completely enveloped mine with warmth and I felt my heart beat a little faster.

"Isobel. I go by Isa."

"Isa." He smiled as he said my name. "Do- do you think I could maybe make it up to you? Maybe buy you another cup of tea?"

I wasn't accustomed to being flirted with and, truth be known, I wasn't entirely sure that's what was happening. Still, something in his eyes seemed sincere and I found myself agreeing.

"I like the white tea at The Nook. You can meet me there this time on Friday," I said, still maintaining a frown but primarily for show.

He looked at his watch. "Twelve twenty-two at the Nook on Friday. I'll be there."

He backed away from me grinning ear to ear. His smile was slightly crooked, pulling up just a little higher on the right and displaying barely crooked teeth. Despite myself, I found such imperfection endearing and I watched him rejoin his friends.

The Nook was a well-known establishment to all students. It was a combination tea house and bookstore that also sold baked goods of questionable legality to a certain clientele. Friday afternoons were generally slow as few students took advantage of the atmosphere to study before the weekend. I arrived at noon and perused the bookshelves. New releases of steamy romance novels called to me from the tabletop displays. I subtly glanced at them as I meandered casually toward the discount book bin.

I looked at my watch. Twelve twenty. What was I doing? How could I honestly think someone so attractive had really invited me out? He probably said it just to save face for kicking me in the back of the head. Or worse, maybe the whole thing was some kind of fraternity prank and there were a bunch of guys hiding behind a bookshelf snickering at me. I shook my head and told myself to stop being ridiculous.

I was reading the back of a confusing-sounding novella that had to do with rainbows and sociopaths when I heard the bell on the front door chime. I looked up and saw the man from two days prior. He was wearing a clean navy-blue polo shirt and khaki pants. His hair was stylishly gelled again and his face was freshly shaven. His eyes met mine and he smiled that crooked smile.

"Hello, Isa." He joined me.

"Luke." I smiled at him. "No frisbees today?"

He chuckled slightly. "No, no. I thought we might get to know each other without giving you second-degree burns and a concussion."

He held out his arm for me to go first and we took our places in the queue to order.

"What do you like?" I asked him.

"I hear the white tea is pretty good," he said, his eyes never leaving the menu board behind the counter.

We chose a table next to a brightly sunlit window and sat with one mug of white tea with honey, one steamy green tea, and a plate of banana pudding cookies (the legal ones) for us to share.

I saw his hands shaking a little as he sipped his tea.

"You didn't think you were going to get this far, did you?" I asked.

"Nope." He shook his head. "I was afraid you had only agreed to meet me to be polite."

"If it makes you feel any better, I thought the same thing about you." I smiled.He laughed a little. "You're beautiful and you always sound so smart in comp two. I thought you would shoot me down on Wednesday and when you didn't, I thought for sure you'd stand me up today."

I was a little shocked. No one besides my dad had ever called me beautiful before.

"Do I seem like such a mean person?" I asked.

"No. But I don't really know you yet either. Do I seem so mean to you?"

"That's a fair point." I nodded in concession. "We have comp two together?"

"Yeah. You always sit up front. I'm always in the back because I'm usually running late from effective speaking."

"What's your major?"

"Architecture. Yours?"

"Undeclared."

I always felt awkward answering that question. I was two years into college at twenty years old and still didn't know what I wanted to do with my life.

"Too tough to choose?" he asked, taking a bite out of a soft, warm cookie.

I nodded.

"What interests you?" he prodded.

"Everything," I answered honestly. "I thought about medicine but I don't think I have enough empathy. I thought about engineering but I'm not that great at math. I don't really like kids so teaching is out, though if I did teach, it would be world history."

"Okay." He smiled. "Let's look at it from another angle. Instead of what interests you, what are you passionate about?"

"Words," I said without hesitation.

"Words?"

"I love to read. Poetry. Novels. Shampoo bottles. I also love to write. I love all of it."

He smiled wide and it made my heart flutter a little.

"So, what about journalism?" he asked.

I shrugged. "The news is depressing and I think I'd be miserable having someone else tell me what I have to write about."

"So be an English major and become a novelist."

"It is really hard to be a successful novelist."

"It's really hard to become a successful architect but that's not going to stop me from trying."

"I see your point but it's also hard to make real money as a writer."

"Would you rather live happy or die rich?"

The complete insouciance with which he posed the question caught me by surprise. I sputtered a little trying to formulate a response, but I couldn't come up with one.

"I don't even know how to answer that." I shook my head. "Maybe I'm not as good with words as I thought."

He laughed a deep belly laugh and I couldn't help myself and joined him. It turned out to be a lovely afternoon. I found myself relaxing and even recited a few of my favorite poems that I had written. The way he looked at me when I was talking made me a little uncomfortable and yet esteemed. I hate to use the cliché that it was as if we were the only two people there but there is no more accurate description. By the time the tea was drunk and the cookies were eaten, we had discussed classes, grades, writers, artists, and families.

As we prepared to leave, he held his arms out with his palms up as if in supplication.

"I'd like to take you out for a full meal if you'll let me."

Despite all of the doubt I had arrived with that day, I really could not think of a reason, not one at all, why I shouldn't spend more time with him.

"I never turn down good Thai food." I shrugged, trying to seem as falsely dispassionate as possible.

The crooked smile stretched broadly across his face and he stood a little straighter.

"Can I have your phone number?" He asked as he held his phone out to me.

I punched my number and saved it to his phone. He immediately sent me a message that simply said *hi*.

I started to save the number and then frowned.

"Is something wrong?" he asked.

"We talked about so much today, but I never got your last name."

"Winter. Lucas Archibald Winter."

"Archibald?" I scrunched up my nose and stifled a giggle.

"Dad lost a bet with Grandpa. And you are Isobel...?"

"Marie Williams."

"Isobel Marie Williams." He held out his hand. "It was nice to meet you."

I shook his hand. "You too Lucas Archibald Winter."

That weekend I was walking a little lighter as I served tables. Even a few of my regulars commented on how I was glowing and my manager said I was practically waltzing. I couldn't help myself. I was giddy in a way I had never felt before.

The following Monday, about seven minutes into my English Composition class, I heard the door open and close softly. I turned slightly in my seat and looked over my shoulder. Lucas Archibald Winter was taking a seat in the back of the room. I had honestly never noticed him sneaking in late before. I think that, because he told me, a little part of me was listening for him. After class, he remained standing next to his seat until I caught up with him.

"Hello again." He smiled a little differently this time, a little more confident.

"Hello again," I said.

"Would you like to sit with me outside for a little bit? No frisbee.'

I agreed.

"So, what are you doing for your persuasive essay?" I asked him.

"Honestly," he said. "I'm cheating a little."

"How so?"

"My morning class is effective speaking. Just so happens that I have to make a persuasive speech this week before the essay is due. My speech is already half done so I'm just going to change it up a little to make the essay."

"So, you're turning in the same assignment for two different classes."

"Essentially. It should give me more time to study for this calculus class that's kicking my butt."

He held the door open for me as we stepped out into the bright sunshine.

"What's your topic?" I asked.

"That mass production of animals for pet stores should be outlawed."

We sat on a bench.

"You mean like puppy mills?" I asked.

"See." He lit up. "Everyone immediately jumps to dogs and cats but what about the other animals? Their so-called breeders are mass production facilities that pump pet stores full of hundreds of thousands of rabbits, rodents, birds, and reptiles with absolutely zero regard for their health, welfare, and eventual ownership. Did you know that most of those animals aren't even covered in the Animal Welfare Act? They have no protection unless they're used in research."

"I didn't know that. You seem pretty passionate about it."

He let out a laugh that was something like a bark. "A little. I promise I'm not one of those crazies that says owning pets is slavery and I do eat meat. I just believe that animals should be treated with respect and dignity, you know?"

The more he talked, the more I enjoyed listening to him. He seemed like such a genuinely kind soul and he was an animal lover.

"What about you? What are you doing for your essay?" he asked.

"Nothing so profound. I'd like to convince people to ride bikes more than drive. For example, my next-door neighbor growing up. She would get up early in the morning and run six miles around the loop of our neighborhood for her health but then get in a car and drive two miles for a single bag of groceries. How many people do you know like that? It's crazy. I don't get it."

He looked contemplative. "But biking isn't always safe. People in cars get angry and stupid around bikers."

"True," I conceded. "But if *enough* people turn to biking, cars will have to either behave safer or municipalities will have to put in more bike lanes like other countries."

"Do you really see that happening in the U.S.?"

"No." I smiled and shook my head. "Not at all. People love their big comfy SUVs and hate exercise. But I don't have to believe it to write one little college essay."

"True." He nodded.

We sat in the sunlight for another twenty minutes before he excused himself for his next class on the other side of campus. I watched him walk away shifting a shoulder bag full of books from one side to the other. I ran my hand through my long red hair and scratched my head. I liked him. I knew I did. Did I really want the distraction of a romantic relationship?

He called me that night and asked if I'd like to split a large pizza with him on Friday instead of Thai food. I said yes. Apparently, I did want the distraction.

Outside of school, I waited tables for two twelve-hour shifts on the weekends. He stocked shelves at the big box store at night after classes. Somehow, we found time to sit together during our afternoon break a few times per week or share a meal or a cup of tea here and there.

One night, we were sitting at a table on the balcony of his apartment with his roommates. We were drinking beer and playing cards. When it was his turn to deal, he fanned the deck and told me to pick a card. I removed the queen of spades. He shuffled the deck.

"Put it back anywhere," he instructed.

I did as I was told and he began to shuffle them again. He had me cut the deck and he took one half and set it aside. He shuffled the other half and began to lay the cards out in groups of four, facing up.

Thinking he was looking for some kind of reaction from me, I maintained the straightest face I could muster and tried to focus on him instead of the cards. He stopped with a little over half of the other cards still in his left hand.

"I'll bet you a kiss the next card I turn over is your card."

I was shocked. It was such an audacious bet but then I realized that while we had been spending our free moments together for around a month, we had never had any remotely romantic expression. We hadn't even had a hug. The most affectionate interaction we had had was a handshake. I didn't know why; I did feel something for him.

I glanced down at the cards he had already placed on the table. The queen of spades looked up at me. I smiled at him.

"Bet," I said.

He grinned wide and promptly flipped the queen face down. His roommates broke out in drunken laughter. So did I. I leaned over and Lucas pressed his lips against mine.

I want to say that it was a magical kiss. I want to say it was intense and perfect. In reality, my anxiety caused my chest to tighten and my stomach to cave in on itself. After having had so many beers, I had to force myself to keep from vomiting on him instead of enjoying the moment. Thankfully, I don't think he noticed.

That night I slept in his bed. In part, it was because I was too intoxicated to drive home safely but mostly because I wanted to be near him. He gave me a t-shirt that was just slightly too big to sleep in and we fell asleep together. I'd be lying if I didn't admit we made love in the morning before I had to go home and change for work.

That was it. We were a match set after that. I no longer fought what I knew was there and accepted him as a major part of my life wholly. That Thanksgiving he came home to meet my family. My father and grandfather put him through a thorough line of questioning before deciding they weren't going to need to threaten his safety. I underwent a similar interrogation from his three sisters at Christmas. Having achieved a stamp of approval from each other's families didn't quite validate our relationship but it did make it seem somehow more real. We weren't just two dating college kids. We were a couple.

Two years after we met, he entered his three semesters of co-op. It was brutal and he was tired. We saw each other much less and most of our interaction was via text message but we held on. It was worth it when one of the architectural firms he was working with offered him a bottom-rung position to get his foot in the door.

A year and a half later I graduated with my bachelor's degree in English and not long after that we moved into an apartment together with a little calico kitten he found at a jobsite. That first year was hard and I honestly wasn't sure if we were going to make it. He still wanted to live like a college bachelor and had mounds of clothes all over the bedroom and left dirty dishes wherever he set them. I was not without fault. I had taken a position writing for an online magazine to pay the bills while working on my first serious novel. I hated it. I was stressed, depressed, and overwhelmed. I released the tension by taking it out on him even though I knew it was wrong. Everything he did upset me. The sound of my voice upset him. It came to a head when we got into a screaming match and he left to stay with his older sister for three days.

"You are such a child!" I had yelled.

"A child? I work all day every day!"

"So do I! I don't want to have to come home and clean up after you!"

"You're home more than I am. Why shouldn't you do most of the cleaning?"

"I'm not your maid!"

"I'm not saying you are but you sit at a desk all day and

you're home more than I am. You're more available to clean than I am."

"So, I don't work as hard as you? Is that what you mean?"

"Kind of." His eyes widened and he regretted it as soon as he said it.

I felt my lower jaw tremble. "I go to the office every day. I come home and cook and clean every night. Every weekend I work on the novel that *you* encouraged me to write. In the morning you put on the laundry that I washed. You come home to the apartment that I cleaned. You eat the meals that I cook and you sit on your ass."

"What? So, I do nothing?"

"Not only do you do nothing, but you go out of your way to make things harder on me by leaving your crap everywhere."

"I live here too. Why shouldn't I be comfortable? And I'm tired when I come home."

I forced my jaw to unclench. "I'm tired too but I still make sure we have a sanitary home. Your comfort will attract roaches and mice."

"I'm not that disgusting."

"Ha!" It was a completely mirthless, cynical sound that I didn't even know I could make.

"If I'm so gross and make things so much harder on you, maybe I shouldn't be here." His voice was low and more angry than sad.

"Maybe you shouldn't."

He left. He didn't even take his coat.

Those three days were pure Hell. We were each too stubborn to reach out first. I was completely unable to focus at work during the day and cried myself to sleep at night. The apartment felt cold, vast, and empty. My chest felt hollow and I tried to rationalize it all by talking to the cat. The morning of the fourth day was a cold, bleak Saturday. I finally set my pride aside and called him to say we needed to talk.

He came home an hour later. He was wearing clothes two sizes too big and I realized his bother-in-law must have been sharing his wardrobe that week. He had a cup of tea from The Nook in each hand. His eyes, which were normally so vibrant, were dark and sunken from lack of sleep and rimmed red from crying. We sat at the kitchen table with our tea and laid out all of our frustration. Voices elevated a few times but we brought them back down. By evening we realized we hadn't eaten all day. We ordered a pizza and continued our discussion and negotiations. By midnight we were both physically and emotionally depleted but all the better for it. We went to bed that night wrapped in each other's arms as if afraid to let go.

The following Friday I came home to a steak dinner already prepared.

"What's the occasion?" I asked eagerly.

He had been talking about the potential for a promotion in the weeks prior to our fight so I had assumed it was official.

"I'm hoping it's a celebration," he said sounding nervous. It was the same nervous note he'd had in his voice when he asked me out for tea all those years ago.

He met me standing in the middle of the living room. He put something soft in my hands, closed them around it, and held my hands in his.

"Being apart last week made me realize that I don't want a life without you in it. The fact that we could spend a day talking about it and working with each other instead of for ourselves makes me believe we can get through anything."

He released my hands. The soft thing was a little black velvet pouch. Shaking, I emptied the contents into my open palm. Out rolled a slightly tarnished gold filigree ring.

"It was Grandma's," he explained.

"It's beautiful," I whispered with what little breath I was able to catch.

He swallowed hard. "Will you be my wife?"

I looked into his eyes. They were pleading but hopeful.

"You're sure?" I asked.

"This is the only thing I have ever been sure of in my life."

He said it with such conviction, such certainty. And me? Was I willing to legally bind myself to him? I already felt like he and I were joined at the soul but was I really ready to say the words 'til death do us part' in front of all of our friends and family? Would I truly mean it if I did?

"Yes," I whispered and nodded as my thoughts returned to the moment. "Yes," I said again more firmly.

In one sweeping motion he lifted me off the ground and spun around on his toes as he pressed his lips to mine. He sat me down, took the ring, and slid it on my finger. It fit like it had no previous owner. I looked at it on my hand. My vision was blurred by tears. They were tears of joy, fear, and excitement.

Our wedding the following fall was simple and small. We had a few dozen of our closest family and friends to a winery outside of town. Two of my cousins stood as my bridesmaids in cornflower blue. His two roommates from college stood beside him. My father was puffed with pride as he walked me down the aisle. When it came time for speeches, the best man clanked his wine glass with a spoon and stood.

"Five years ago," he began. "Luke pointed to a pretty redheaded girl walking across the quad and told me that he was working up the nerve to talk to her. I know my best friend and I know he can be shy so two days later when I saw her sitting outside, I threw a frisbee in her direction just to give him a little nudge. I didn't, however, remember that he is a clutz until after he kicked her in the head and tripped over her." The room filled with laughter. "My arm still hurts from time to time from where he punched me after he finally talked to her. But after their first date, I would have let him punch me every day to see him that happy." Everyone aww-ed. "So, I'd like to take full credit for today and say that I've never seen a better couple." Friends and family applauded as Luke and I hugged him.

It was two months later when I began waking up in the middle of the night to vomit. I was a perpetually cold person but around two in the morning, like clockwork, I'd feel like a boiler oven. I'd run to the bathroom to vomit and feel my temperature plummet as soon as my stomach was empty. Luke, who could sleep through a car crashing through the house, never noticed.

I kept telling myself it was a weird PMS symptom. I was due for my period so that had to be it. I was on birth control, after all. When I entered week two of night sweats and vomiting and I still hadn't started, my denial was almost impossible to maintain. I left work early one day and stopped by the pharmacy. The family planning aisle was an overwhelming assortment of condoms, ovulation predictors, prenatal vitamins, and fertility supplements. When I located the pregnancy tests, I selected the two that looked easiest to read. I felt myself looking around cautiously and checking each aisle as I passed. I was afraid someone I knew might see me. It was almost like I was ashamed of needing them. Why? I was a married woman and even if I wasn't it still was nothing to be ashamed of. Women buy pregnancy tests every day. Yet I still used the self-checkout just to be sure no judgmental eyebrows would rise.

At home, the first test showed a plus sign before I even had a chance to set the timer. My heart tried to break through my chest as I prayed that meant the test was faulty. I don't think I breathed for the full two minutes before the second test displayed, very clearly, the word 'pregnant.' The whole room went dark. I could neither see nor hear anything. I stood, feeling like my world was collapsing around me. My chest caved in and left no space for my heart to beat or my lungs to fill with air.

Pregnant.

I finally pulled myself together enough to stumble into the kitchen and put the kettle on the stove. I put a chamomile tea bag into my favorite mug while wishing we had something much stronger in the cupboard. The kettle whistled. I filled my mug and sat at the table feeling like nothing in the kitchen – in the world – was real.

Pregnant.

The tea had barely had enough time to steep when I heard the apartment door open.

"Hi, honey! You're home early."

Luke sounded in high spirits as I heard him shuffle down

the hall. Next, I heard the bathroom door close... and almost immediately open back again. He appeared at the juncture between the living room and the kitchen holding the two pregnancy tests. His eyes were wide but his expression was impossible to read.

"These are real?" he asked.

I nodded. I could feel my eyes start to burn and blood rushed to my face.

"But you're on the pill." It may be my imagination, but his tone almost sounded accusatory as if I had been lying about being on birth control for all these years.

"It's not a hundred percent effective. We're in the less than one percent." I wasn't even looking him in the eye. I couldn't.

He nodded solemnly. He set the tests on the counter, retrieved a mug from the cabinet, and sat across from me at the table with his own cup of tea. We sat in silence for what felt like hours. I partly wished I could read his mind. I didn't know what to say. I didn't know how he felt. I didn't know how *I* felt. Not entirely. I know I felt guilty. I felt like I had trapped us. I felt like now it was my fault that we had to choose whether or not we wanted to be parents. We had never even discussed it before. It was my fault that we may have to change everything about our lives. Maybe we could give it to a stranger through an agency. Would I be able to do that after having grown it inside me for nine months? I didn't really like kids but maybe it would be different if it was mine. Maybe we should end it now before it had a consciousness. My head was spinning and I felt sick. The only thing I could be certain of was that our lives were different from this point forward.

"We're going to need a bigger apartment," he said, finally breaking the agonizing silence.

I felt my face get hot again.

"You want to keep it?" I finally choked.

"I think I do. I always knew I wanted a family with you. I just didn't know it would be so soon. Do you want to keep it?"

I felt tears rolling down my face as I tried to maintain some semblance of composure. I looked down at my hands. They were shaking. He laid his left hand on top of my right to steady it.

"I don't know," I whispered.

"That's fair," he said. His tone was so even and understanding. How was he not freaking out? "Let's talk about this. It's kind of something we both have to agree on."

We talked and sipped our tea. We laid out all of our options. We looked at the pros and cons of each. We looked at our budget and financial options. Eventually, I calmed enough to munch on some cheese and bread for dinner.

"So, what are we going to call it if it's a girl?" he asked, our conversation finally reaching a conclusion.

"Ruth," I said.

"You want our daughter to be beaten up every day of her life?"

I shrugged. "I think it's beautiful."

That night, he fell asleep with my head on his right arm and his left hand on my belly. I was too scared to sleep. Having a baby wasn't just having a baby. It was bringing another life into the world. That would be a life that we were forever responsible for. We had spent hours discussing it but discussion and reality were two very different things.

The following Wednesday I had an ultrasound. It was uncomfortable as they slid the probe inside me and moved it around. I squeezed Luke's hand mostly for the comfort of knowing he was there. They said I measured at six weeks and two days. There was no heartbeat but the ultrasound technician said not to worry because the whole heartbeat at twenty-one days thing was a gross generalization. I was told to return in two weeks.

Over the next thirteen days, we would randomly bounce names off each other. Candace. Anthony. Emily. Charlie. I could see Luke getting excited and he began looking at new apartments. He would detour down the infant aisle at the grocery store and talked about seeing what his sisters had left from when his nieces and nephews were little. His enthusiasm was infectious. I wasn't nearly as excited as him; the prospect of motherhood still terrified me. But I couldn't help but be happy at his excitement. All the while, however, I was getting sicker. My midnight purges turned into morning sickness then vomiting every time I would eat something. I was miserable and fairly certain I was losing weight.

Finally, the day came for the second ultrasound. This one was performed with the transducer on my belly, thankfully. I measured at six weeks and two days with no heartbeat. Something was wrong. I don't remember what was said. I was deaf and numb. Luke had lost all color in his face. I was sent to the university hospital where I had some blood drawn. We didn't speak a word. There were more doctors and some shaking heads. It's all mostly a blur. I was given a pill and told not to go to work for the next two days. Lucas called off work and held my hand as I had the worst menstruation of my life.

We tried to watch TV and pretend it wasn't happening, but it was painful – emotionally and physically – beyond words. The following morning, I woke with none of the nausea I had had over the previous weeks. It was over. Our families never even knew I was pregnant.

I accepted the miscarriage as part of nature. It was all I could do. I hadn't been eager to be a mother at that stage in my life, but I had come to some form of acceptance of the idea. I wondered what it would look like and what it would grow up to be. I saw happy mothers with their children at the store and thought that could have been me. But it wasn't and nothing would change that.

Lucas, on the other hand, was devastated. He took another week off of work but mostly used it to mull around the apartment, not even bothering to get dressed. His heart was broken and I couldn't mend it. It was another few weeks before I could convince him to seek help. He started counseling and I even went to a few sessions so we could work through it together. While it strengthened us, he was never quite the same after.

Every night we fell asleep holding hands or rubbing feet. The constant reassurance became a necessary comfort, especially to him. Christmas and Thanksgiving hit hard when family members asked when we were going to have children. Even I was panged but we pulled through. As he said, we could get through anything.

Then February came. He was at a job site in a semi-rural area about eight miles from the apartment. I had worked on my article from home that day. It had rained that morning which then froze as the temperature dropped throughout the day. Around four in the afternoon, marble-sized flakes of snow began falling. At six he called to apologize for leaving work late but promised he was on his way home.

Seven o'clock came. Then eight. He wasn't answering my calls but he never used the phone while driving and he could have still been trying to find his way home. At nine I made a cup of tea to calm my nerves. By ten I left the undrunk tea, grabbed my keys, and headed out. Once I had left the main suburban thoroughfare, I could hardly tell what was road and what wasn't. The layer of snow was thick and dry and gusts sent up clouds of it that made it difficult to see. Beneath the snow, a sheet of ice covered the asphalt causing my car to slip or spin out spots.

Then, maybe five miles from home, my headlights caught a flash of bright blue. I stopped my car and jumped out. His sedan was wrapped around a pole on the driver's side. The window was smashed and he was partly covered in snow.

"Lucas?" I whispered.

I touched him, hoping to feel the warmth of life but he was as cold as the wind. I'm still not sure if I actually made sound when I screamed. Maybe nothing came out. Maybe it was absorbed by the snow. Maybe I blocked it out. But I was hoarse when I finally collected myself enough to call nine-one-one and try to explain to the operator where we were.

A kind officer wrapped a blanket around me and sat me in the back of his cruiser while they cut Lucas out of the remains of his car. I couldn't feel the cold. I couldn't hear the emergency vehicles. It was like I was watching everything on a screen with the sound turned off. Eventually, entrusting the rest of the vehicle to a tow truck driver and another officer, the nice cop drove me home.

When I closed the apartment door behind me, I looked around with eyes that could not see anything. The couch wasn't real nor the cat that sat on it. The carpet looked more like a wispy cloud than something I could walk on. Everything had a watery fog around it. Lucas was gone. The last six years – our next fifty years – gone. Stolen from me. My eyes eventually came to rest on the now-cold mug of tea on the table. It had all started with a cup of tea.

8

The Resurrection of Magic

There were bodies lying openly on the street. Most had fly-infested wounds. Dried blood smattered their skin and the ground around them. Their bellies were round and bloated with early stages of decay. They stood no chance against what had happened here. Some of the men appeared to be militia. They had died with their guns in hand in an attempt to defend their homes. Others had the bodies of women- presumably their wives- draped over them like blankets. The children were lined up undressed in neat little rows in front of the church. It was as if the proximity would hasten their little souls into heaven. One thing was certain, she who was responsible for this atrocity should be delivered to Lucifer on a flaming chariot, but she feared no such thing. This had been done by man on her command no amount of penance could erase this from one's chapter in God's book.

We continued to walk the street in silent awe and horror. Some men stayed back to search the bodies for survivors while others explored the dwellings. Not even the pets had been spared. Dogs lay in bloody heaps in the gutters while rats gnawed on their corpses. I heard one of my companions vomiting behind me.

"Stomach up, Lad. Something tells me this isn't the worst of it," I shouted over my shoulder.

Thane ran up behind me and put his hand on my shoulder. "There are no girls."

"What do you mean?" I turned to him.

"The children. They are all male." His eyes were wide.

I returned to the church. Just as he had said, all of the naked little bodies were boys.

"What is this?" The heartbreak in Thane's voice was audible. But he knew exactly what we were facing.

"Sir!" Gavin ran to me as fast as he could while lugging a forty-pound pack. He was huffing heavily and looked as if he was trying not to cry. "The field. You have to see for yourself."

I followed him with true fear in my heart. These were hardened men and they were breaking around me. As soon as the field entered my view, I saw it. I knew true horror in that moment.

A perfect circle had been scorched into the ground. Twenty-three stakes had been driven into the soil. Twenty-three little bodies were charred to the wood. Some of the remnants of the faces still had contorted looks of terror and agony. Twenty-three sacrificed virgins. Off to the side of this macabre display, some of my men were crying, some were vomiting, and some just sat in stunned silence. These poor tortured innocents were a warning to me and my men. If we did not stop our pursuit, no one would be spared. No one would come between her and her power. But I could not stop. I was bound by blood.

My prey was Mab, the Mother of Magic. More than half a millennia ago she vanished from Earth and was forced into exile under the old Saxon's land shortly after Charlemagne had destroyed it. Her son, the great wizard, Merlin, had cast his greatest spell. As with all gods, Mab's power came from belief in (and more so fear of) her abilities. Her struggles began with the forced conversion of the people to Christianity. Merlin, with the help of Mab's sister, the Lady in the Lake, bewitched the water so whoever drank it would forget about Mab entirely. As the spell spread, Mab and the Lady faded away almost completely. Before he died in 1002 at one hundred and forty-six years old, he left an enchanted knife with the Lady. He knew that one day, she and Mab would return and there would be no one strong enough to cast the spell again. The blade would release the magic contained within Mab to spread across the world with the wind. There would be no guarantee who would learn to tame it, but at least it would no longer be hers and hers alone.

He didn't know when it would happen, but he did accurately predict her return. Just less than a hundred years ago, a macabre group found a library in a forgotten castle. That's where they found her book. In just a short time, they had formed a cult, fed her with their worship, nourished her with their sacrifices, and brought her back. As she gained strength, she cut a bloody path across Europe, reminding people who she was and that they should fear her. The more news of her return spread, the stronger she became.

You may be wondering at this point what it all has to do with me. Merlin had died centuries ago with no magic left to speak of. The Great Wizard was my ancestor. It was believed that Merlin had no children. No one knows this fact is a lie conjured for protection. His beloved Nimue had given birth in secret on the Isle of Avalon. Though it pained them to do it, they left the child there to be raised by the nuns to keep him safe from Mab. After Mab's disappearance, they decided it was best not to let the child's paternity be known to anyone except the Lady of the Lake. She would need to know who the blade belonged to when the time came. One night, Nimue crept to the water's edge and introduced her son to the sea that surrounded Avalon. She hoped that there was just enough strength left in the Lady to hear her.

With the return of Mab came the return of the Lady. When she was strong enough, the Lady found my Great, Great Grandfather as he gathered water from the well and presented him with the blade, his quest, and basic instruction of how to control whatever magic was within him. And so, it has been passed down as each generation has failed. I have no sons. It was up to me.

I felt something brush against my leg. I looked down and saw a soot-smudged tabby gently pleading at my feet. A survivor. A witness. I picked up the cat. It smelled of smoke and earth. I knew what I was about to do would drain me. As Mab's power grew, so did mine but I was generations removed from Merlin. I took a deep breath and looked into the cat's eyes. I looked past the muted yellow rings into the black pointed pools of the center. Deeper. Deeper. Until all around me was black. I searched the darkness until I saw them. The mass and might of the King's army was laying siege to the tiny village. The villagers fought to save their homes with knives, swords, and a few guns, but mostly farm implements. They didn't stand a chance.

I continued my search. I looked beyond the rape and slaughter until I saw her. The Mother of Magic was leaning over the shoulder of a man in a general's uniform. She was whispering in his ear. Her long, white hair billowed with the breeze as she spoke. Her eyes, blue as a pool of clean water, touched everything they saw with evil. Even from the safety of a cat's memory, I could feel her hatred and I was almost certain she looked straight at me. She instructed the general to spare only those who would join her army. I heard the general order the men to take whatever food and provisions they would need to move on to Bethany.

Somewhere in the distance, I heard a voice say "Captain?" The village around me started to fade. "Captain?" The voice was a little louder now. I felt a jolt and all at once, the darkness and everything around me disappeared. I stood amongst a few of my men, holding a very confused cat. I crumbled to my knees and dropped the animal as I gasped and desperately tried to catch my breath. The air was cold but I could feel it bring life to my lungs.

"Captain? Are you alright?" Thane's voice seemed distant for as near as he stood.

"Bethany," I coughed. "They are marching to Bethany."
"The ground is still warm. We are not too far behind. If we make a good pace, we may catch them."

I shook my head. "No. We must bury the dead."

"Sir, that will take the rest of the day," he protested.

"We are not going to leave them here for the crows and rats to feast. They are brave people who fought and gave their lives for their families. They have earned a burial."

He nodded curtly. "Yes, sir."

I felt a soft rub and heard a gentle purr. "And find food for the damn cat!" I ordered.

The men spent the remainder of the day and into the next getting the girls off the pikes, scouring the homes and shops for bodies and supplies, and digging trenches. I knew Mab would be gaining ground. I did not care. I needed time to think and these people needed a proper burial.

Three days later we came upon the remains of Bethany. Laid before us was total devastation. Trees were not just charred; they were bent at the base and lay level on the ground. Crops were flattened and laid waste as if the locusts had come. It was nearly biblical. It was Mab mocking me. Taunting me. She demonstrated raw power that I could never match.

"Where are they, sir?" Thane asked.

I shook my head and we wandered through the devastation. Not a single body was found. Her power was growing.

We made camp in near silence. Sitting around the fires and eating old bread, we could feel the fear that was settling over the camp. It hung like a choking fog that would not – could not – be ignored. If her power could do this now, what hope did we have to stop her?

A scout jogged to my fire breathing heavily. "Sir. They are headed west on a straight path."

"Thank you. That'll be all," I dismissed him.

He nodded and left towards another fire and supper.

"West? What is in the West?" Thane asked, perplexed.

I knew the answer. I had known for some time but feared to admit it. This was only confirmation. "Brecilien Forest." I poured some of my water onto a piece of stale bread and some molded cheese on the plate on the ground for the cat.

"Brecilien? Why would she go there?"

"Because within lies the lake her sister calls home. Beyond that is Avalon. Her sister will either join her or perish. With The Lady out of the way, nothing can stop her from reaching Avalon."

"What is in Avalon of such value?"

"It is where the last of her magical creatures went to die. Fairies, elves, and even unicorns' remains are there. She will create a throne, resurrect them, and rule a new age of magic."

My men looked at me, mouths agape.

"How do you know this, sir?" Gavin asked with hesitation.

I shook my head. "I do not know how. But I do know it to be fact."

In truth, I knew it was my connection to her through magic that made me so sure. I could feel her as well as she could feel me. Just as I could feel my power grow as hers grew. I could feel her emotions and motivations and I knew that when she focused, she could read my mind.

The next day we marched. And the next. We knew Mab's army was far ahead of us but how close they were to Brecilien Forest, I could not be sure. My only certainty was that The Lady of the Lake still lived. She had magic too and I could feel her though much fainter than her sister.

On the third day we crested the final hill. One hundred and

eighteen men stood behind me. More than a thousand lined the forest before us. I scanned them all quickly, searching for the General and the one who whispered in his ear. I did not have long to search. He stepped out in front of his mem, fearless in his stance. Normally, he would have been my superior officer, but not that day. That day we were on opposing sides of the war.

The sky was grey and lifeless. There was no sun or wind or birds. The men behind me held their breath. It may have been my imagination but I could hear their hearts thumping and cracking their breast bones. Otherwise, all was still.

Shaking slightly, I stepped forward. "Mab!" I called. My voice carried over the earth and bounced off the trees below. "Show yourself!"

The general's body started to shimmer like heat from a sun-baked rock. A white light started at the tips of his fingers and moved to his chest. Then, as if he was being parted from his ghost, she stepped from his body. She had been hiding inside him, attempting to use his thoughts to mask her plans from me. It had not worked.

She walked to the middle of the grassland between us. "Grandson! Come to me!"

I stepped forward to meet her but a hand on my shoulder pulled me back. I turned to face Thane. He looked grave. We had played together as boys. We have fought together as men. When Mab's forces grew, he did not hesitate to follow me across Europe to stop her. My right hand. My best friend. Though he knew what I had to do, he wanted to save my life just as he had done so many times before.

I patted his hand and gave him a smile with a short nod. It

was part to be reassuring. It was part in acknowledgment of his fear. But mostly it was a goodbye.

I looked out over my troops. They all wore the same face of both foreboding and acceptance. They all feared the death that awaited them but accepted it on behalf of the cause. I didn't know what to say to them. They had followed me to this hill. Their loyalty was invaluable. I owed them my life a hundred times over. I only hoped they knew that as I descended the hill.

Though I met her for the first time it felt as if we were simply family that had been parted for some time. We stood an arm's length apart with a narrow stream of water flowing between us. I had been following her for years. I had played this moment in my dreams a thousand times. Now, as I stood before her, I felt like a child awaiting the switch. All preparedness was gone. I stood tall and tried to present a strong front, but my stomach betrayed me and I fought to keep the contents down.

"How bold you are to face me. My power grows. I could tear you apart with only a thought." A strong wind kicked. Her long white hair blew in fury and I saw some of her men bracing themselves against it.

"Tricks and intimidation," I stated with much more confidence than I felt. "If your magic alone could kill, you would not need an army and I would not be standing here." She glowered. "You have an army that is loyal out of fear. My men are loyal for love. Love of me, the families they protect, and their country. One hundred of the best marksmen in Europe want you dead. They will gladly fire on you if I command it."

"Ha!" she spat. "As if I could be killed by bullets and bayonets."

"Maybe not. But they can cause you injury. Will your army be so loyal if they see you weak?"

She glanced at the general from the corner of her eye and emitted a low growl. She held her arms out to her sides with her palm raised. She then drew her hands together over her head forming a wide arc. As she did so, a bubble of pure ice formed around us, encasing us in a frozen dome.

"No armies," she said with a look of sincere satisfaction. "No men. Just us."

The only other sound was the trickling of the water in the stream between us.

"More tricks," I said, trying to sound unimpressed. "Tell me, Mab, will you have the power to raise your creatures if you reach Avalon?"

"Enough of them," she nodded confidently. "With my sister's magic and yours combined with mine. They will go into the world and remind people that magic is real. It lives and grows. As people remember, I will gain strength and awaken more. Magic will retake its rightful place in the world."

"To what end?"

"Theirs." She gestured widely around us. "I was a good queen. A kind queen. I did not hurt those who did not seek to harm me or my children. I did not command obedience or sacrifice from humans. I helped them when asked for it. We of magic lived quietly – peacefully – alongside humans." Her expression became dark. Her blue eyes turned to black. "Then the Christians came. They slaughtered those who followed me or forced them to convert. They captured and enslaved magical beings and drove them into hiding. We were persecuted. We were hunted like rabbits. I watched my children and my kingdom disintegrate. I should not have been so trusting of humans. You so readily destroy each other. I should have known you would destroy my people. This time will be different." Her beautiful face contorted into something like a smile but conveyed nothing but malice. "Kindness has left me now. Their descendants will know my pain. They will watch their families be torn apart. They will follow us or die. Magic will take its place and reign over all."

I found myself feeling sympathy for Mab. In the centuries of her absence, she had been made into a villain. Merlin had been born to lead the people back to magic. But she had killed those he loved the most to try to control him. And he resented her. He fought her. Her acts of desperation became her downfall. I understood now. A part of my heart went out to her. But I could not stand by while hundreds of thousands of people paid for the crimes of their ancestors regardless of how many hundreds of years of resentment she felt.

"You do not have to kill," I said.

"No," she replied. "I do not have to. But I will."

I pulled Merlin's knife from my belt but my arm froze with the point just centimeters from her face.

"You haven't the power," she said serenely. "But you could. Join me, Grandson. Take your place in the world of magic."

I tried to force my hand forward. It would not move. "No."

"Then die as they will but take comfort in knowing your power will be added to ours."

I heard a rush of water. The gentle stream was overflowing with great force. Our dome of ice was filling. My hand still would not budge but Mab was waving her arms trying to melt the ice or break the dome, becoming more frantic as the water rose. She could not drown but she was trapped. I felt the force on my arm release and I dropped the knife. I was floating near the peak of the dome, my boots six feet from the ground. I took a deep breath and dove. The water was surprisingly clear as I searched. I would find that knife or drown.

Suddenly, before my eyes appeared a beautiful woman. Her eyes were the same crystal blue as Mab's. Her dark green dress and long black hair flowed as if made of the water that surrounded us. The Lady of the Lake. She held the dome in place. She was keeping her sister distracted.

I heard a gentle voice. "My magic must not be used to help her. If I must die again, so be it, but not for the sake of revenge." She pressed the knife into my right hand.

I looked up and saw Mab with her hands against the dome, trying to will it away. My lungs burned for oxygen as I pulled together all of my power. I had never used it this way, but somehow, I knew what I had to do. I released the magic, using it to propel me forward with incredible force. I hit Mab hard, knocking her head against the ice with a dull thud that was audible even under water. She was stunned just enough to allow me to slide the blade through her ribs, to the left of her spine, and into her heart. Her body seized like a wood plank. Inky black blood poured from the wound and mixed with the swirling water until all was dark. Just when I thought I would lose consciousness from holding my breath, the dome disappeared, the water was no longer contained, and I hit the ground.

When I woke, I lay on the ground on my back with Cat purring on my chest and my men surrounding me.

"Where is she," my voice was a harsh, croaking sound.

"Carried downstream," Thane answered. "Her army has scattered."

Behind his head, I saw a butterfly flutter. No, not a butterfly. It was far too big.

"We have to go," I forced myself to my feet, swooning a little as I regained control of my body.

"Why?" asked Gavin. "Mab is dead."

"Not all of her."

We marched a full day through Brecilien Forrest. As we passed the lake, I searched the waters for a sign of The Lady but saw none. That night we made camp on the bank of the Sea on the other side of the trees. I slept deep and dreamed of elves pointing arrows at me, bows drawn at the ready. My rifle melted from my hand and into the dirt. It was useless against so many.

The next morning, I woke to see Thane and several others staring out over the vast, open water.

"What is it?" I joined them.

Thane pointed to a tiny wooden boat that was drifting straight for us. "No oars or a sail but it does not move in the same direction as the water flows."

"At the center of the sea is Avalon. She has sent the boat for me," I explained.

"Mab is dead."

"Not Mab." I turned back to my bedroll. I packed my rifle, some bread, and extra ammunition in a sack. After my dream, I knew it was a useless act, but I was a soldier after all. I patted Cat's head before I stepped into the boat, now resting on the bank.

"Captain, how should we follow you?" Gavin asked.

"You cannot follow." I shook my head. "I go alone. You must guard this shore against any others. Do you understand? You must not allow anyone else to reach Avalon."

The men nodded.

The boat carried me out into the water. I knew it flowed but could not see it move. A thick fog enveloped me as I lost sight of the men on the shore. I could not see or hear anything. I became disoriented. I could not see the sun to determine time or direction. I knew it was magic. I could feel it. It was put into place to protect the island. I do not know how much time passed before the fog cleared. The boat came to rest on a rocky shore. I was drawn to a treacherous path up a cliff. At the top, lush, green grass spread before me. Fairies like the one I had seen behind Thane's head tended to flowers while what I thought might be gnomes replaced stones in the road. They all stared at me with murderous eyes as I passed them toward the stone temple at the center of the island.

In the great hall of the temple, The Lady sat acrest the water of a marble fountain. A queen on her throne.

"Enter." She gestured to me with open arms.

"Mab's magic lives in you." I stood before her.

"Yes."

"Will you finish her work?"

Her features darkened. "Will you force me to?"

9

My Knight

I cannot take it anymore. The lies. The whispers. The secrets. They keep swirling in my mind like an unknown creature flapping in the night. I remember him telling me he would never leave me. I remember the words he spoke to me on our wedding night. "I shall never vanish. You are my sanity. You make me whole and my love for you is eternal."

It pains me now to think that I had once been irresponsible enough to believe those words. I was young and ignorant. I had been so captivated by the tone in which he spoke those words to me that I had actually believed him. But they were lies. All lies. He was a notorious addict to the whores that plagued the village, useless concubines that made my life hell. The most painful truth about them is that I have learned he plans to strip me of my title of his Lady and replace me with one of them just days from now when our child is born.

The only thing he truly loves is the heir I bear. But after, I will be useless. Once he has what he truly desires, my duty as his wife will be obsolete.

How could he do it? I do not understand how he can forget the love I bore him. What of the son that is now growing in my belly? He has no right to deny the family he has given birth to. Yet this does not stop his habits. The brandy and whores are apparent more frequently now than before.

Perhaps it is because he relishes the attention his beautiful looks present him with. But he had been such a strong knight when I had met him. Giving in to such temptations had not occurred to me at the time of our courting. I had been naive. I had not seen these troubles until we went to the king's annual Winter Ball. There we stood arm in arm amongst the other Lords and Ladies. But not one of them would look upon my face or listen to my lips. They whispered of other women and brandy and wine when my back was turned.

That night, I confronted my Lord Knight in our chamber. He told me that rumors were oft carried with the breeze but that did not make them true. He told me he had not, nor would he ever keep secrets from me. I was content with this and that night we made love under a moonless sky.

When I awakened the next morning, I caught him kissing a servant girl on the cheek before leaving. I called the girl into my chambers and she confessed to having been with my husband on several occasions. I did not confront my Lord again for fear of more lies and deceit. I did watch closely, however. I noticed the way women looked at him. Hope and secret knowledge fill their eyes. I now watch them from my window. They slip out through the back garden. Unbeknownst to them their presence is known to me.

I do not chide my Lord Husband. I pretend to be the same foolish young girl I had once been. I need not speak to him nor look at him in an angry manner. 'Tis better to get even, rather than angry. In merely a few days I will bring forth new life, if only for a short while. My lord husband will know what it is to lose something - someone - you treasure. My belly will see to his love, my hand shall see to his loss.

10

The Most Terrifying Question

"Will you marry me?"

Is there a more terrifying question in the English language? Is there a more terrifying question in *any* language? 'Til death do you part is far longer than I think most people realize. To agree to pledge eternity to someone is a lot to ask.

Being female, I am supposed to live for my wedding day. I am supposed to spend every available moment planning the dress, the flowers, the music, and maybe even have a scrapbook of magazine clippings by the age of twelve. In high school I watched my peers plan their lives with boys they had been dating for less than a year. Some of them did wed these boys. Children.

For one day their princess fantasy was a reality. They had their gown and Prince Charming. All eyes of friends and family were on them. But a wedding is different than a marriage and nearly all of these unions ended in divorce by the time we were thirty. Some were due to infidelity. Some were just pure unhappiness; the plan they had made was a stark contrast to reality.

Some had children caught in the middle. Nearly all had bitter endings.

Will you marry me? Will you legally bind yourself to me? Will you promise in front of God and everyone we love that you will never leave me?

His eyes were nervous and his voice was shaky when he spoke those words. Was he as unsure as me? Or did he only fear rejection? If he is unsure, why would he ask? If I reject him, will it break his heart?

"When you know, you know," my friend had said of her own engagement.

But I don't know. I *think* we love each other now. But I don't know what will be ten years from now. I don't know who I will be or what I will want. I don't know if he is going to be abusive or neglectful.

In the conflict of nature vs. environment, some things will reign. People grow and change with time. It is the nature of humanity. Will we change together or will we grow apart?

"It is a leap of faith!" my friend had said.

Faith in what? God? Ten thousand children are going to starve to death tonight. War and pestilence plague nearly eight billion people. I think God has more important things to worry about than my love life. Faith in our love? How can I have faith in something I've never known or felt before? Endorphins and hormones are excellent at altering your mindset and blinding you to reality. I watched my friends and former classmates fall victim to such things. What am I supposed to have faith in?

Will you marry me? Will you be mine forever? I feel as if I am entering a life of voluntary servitude. The vows state love and honor to be sure but many of the weddings I have been to recite love, honor, and *obey*. I am not a dog, a slave, or any other type of servant. I absolutely will not make such a proclamation.

I feel as if my mind is made up. I feel as if I know my answer. But my heart will not fall in line.

I love waking up to him every morning. I love talking about our day every evening. I love sitting in silence with him. I love the way he smells. I love the way my hand fits inside his. I love the way he looks at me. I love our existence together.

So, now, here he is, on one knee, waiting for me to answer, "Will you marry me?"

11

I don't know; I'm just typing

There is a hook by the door where I hang my keys. Today, his keys are hanging there instead. I look around the kitchen. That is his laptop on the table. That is his coffee mug in the sink. Those are his socks on the living room floor and he has left the toilet seat up. I wander into the bedroom and see his watch on the nightstand on the side of the bed he often sleeps. It's the side of the bed he is sitting on now and taking off his boots. That's when I realized that after all of the years we have danced around each other and denied each other, we still ended up here. Together. We share a space and a life. He may not live here, but we have created something in this house.

He looks up and smiles. at me. "Hi, Hun. What do you want

to do for dinner?"

Such a mundane question to carry so much meaning.

12

A Breakup

We were all seated together in the living room. My husband, Matthew, and I sat on opposite ends of the sofa. Meanwhile, his best friend, Chris, and Chris's girlfriend, Ashley, sat almost on top of each other on the loveseat.

I liked Chris. He was a solid, down-to-earth kind of man. He was raised in the same old-English manners that I was. Clean yourself up before calling on a neighbor. Don't sit unless invited to, no matter how well you know your hosts. Don't swear in polite company. However, for all of this, he hunted, fished, worked on cars, and was generally rough; two sides of the same coin.

As for what he saw in Ashley... I couldn't figure it out. She was eleven years his junior – of legal age, mind you – but far less mature than girls her age ought to be. She wore so much makeup that I wasn't sure if I could actually recognize her without it. She cursed constantly without thought, regardless of who was around to hear it. She did this while chewing gum which, despite myself, I likened to a painted cow chewing its cud. She never joined him in his hiking treks (she might get dirty) or hunting (she wasn't a murderer) or even in the garage (her nails!).

I just couldn't understand the attraction but whenever she was around, Matthew and I put on our best smiles and played the good hosts.

This particular Saturday was cold and wet. They had stopped by to borrow Matthew's good camera. I didn't bother to ask why. I was sure it had something to do with Ashley's latest ambition to become an Instagram model. I shuddered at the thought.

"Why don't you help me dig the camera out of the closet? I'm pretty sure it's tucked in all of last year's hiking gear." Matthew rose.

"Oh, God. We'll never find it." Chris laughed as he followed my husband into the spare bedroom.

Ashley and I were alone together, the only sound was the chomping of her cud. I racked my brain for some common ground to break the tension.

"So," I said. "Did you have a good birthday?"

I vaguely recalled Chris had asked for restaurant recommendations.

She sighed in exaggerated boredom. "It was okay. Chris took me to Charred for dinner and gave me this." She held out her arm to show me a silver station bracelet with six little diamonds spaced around it. She sighed again. "He knows I prefer gold, especially rose gold, but this is pretty, I guess.

One day maybe he'll get it. Either that or this is proof that he doesn't really love me."

My jaw dropped. Charred was an upscale steakhouse downtown. Matthew and I had gone for our anniversary and for just the two of us the bill totaled more than three-hundred dollars. I examined the band around her wrist. Sure, the diamonds were small but they were *supposed* to be. There was no way he had spent less than two-hundred dollars on it. Doing a quick tally in my head, Chris had spent an easy five-hundred dollars on her that night. He was a computer wizard who worked in the basement of a large company. He made decent money but that was still a large chunk of change.

I laughed slightly. "You're joking. Right?"

"Not at all. He could have taken me away for the weekend or at least bought me something nicer than this." She flicked her wrist slightly. "He promised to do better at Christmas."

"What is wrong with you?" I blurted out; all manners had gone.

She looked stunned for a moment. "What do you mean?"

"If you equate money with love, do us all a favor and break up with my friend before you bankrupt him and break his heart."

Her eyes narrowed. "If he loves me, he will do what it takes to keep me happy."

"Going into debt for you is not proof that he loves you. On mornings when I have to wake up before Matthew, he gets up when I do to have coffee with me before I leave. That's love. When my car broke down, he took a day off of work to fix it even though I could have easily taken it to a mechanic. That's love. I pack his lunch every night and we listen to each other complain about work every day even though we don't understand half of what the other says. That's love. What you want isn't love. You want a bank with a good dick." I couldn't believe the word came out of my mouth as soon as I said it but I did not regret it.

"Are you going to let her talk to me like that?" She was red-faced and looking past me.

I turned and saw Chris and Matthew standing in the hallway with the camera gear. Chris looked like a frightened animal as his eyes darted between us.

Finally, he turned to Matthew and said, "I think we'd better go."

Matthew nodded.

I stood as Ashley stomped out the front door with Chris in tow. Matthew wrapped his arms around me and kissed my forehead.

"I love you too," he said.

I hadn't realized I had been shaking until I stopped. My husband was warm and strong and it steadily calmed me.

Later that evening we were sitting in our joint office space. He played a game on his computer while I sat in my favorite over-stuffed chair reading a book with a cup of tea. There was a knock on the door. He paused his game and I looked up from my book. Matthew went to the door while I stood in the hall. Chris stepped in.

"I'm sorry for not calling first," he said.

"No worries," Matthew said. "Come in and have a seat."

Chris stepped into the living room but remained standing. He nodded to me.

"What's up?" Matthew asked. "Can I get you a drink?"

"No thanks. I just had a quick question."

"Shoot."

"As my best friends—" he started.

I swallowed hard. I was sure he was going to snap at me for insulting his girlfriend.

His face split into a smile. "Why on earth didn't you warn me about that crazy woman *before* I spent all that money?"

I hadn't expected that. I stepped forward. "You mean, you're not mad at me?"

"The only reason to be mad is the fact that you two let me waste more than a year and thousands of dollars on that gold digger. Honestly, one of you should have slapped me and told me to snap out of it."

13

Muerte, New Mexico

When my wife died, I made the fateful decision to uproot myself from New York. She had been struck in a crosswalk on her way to get coffee before work. Without her, the city seemed like such an overcrowded yet desolate place. People were everywhere like cockroaches scurrying from building to building. Our tiny apartment felt like the walls had moved inward and our once cozy little place became a prison cell. Worst of all was her ghost haunting every space. There was the corner where I had been staring at my phone while walking and walked right into her, fate bringing us together. There was the restaurant where we had our first date and the park across the street where I had proposed. At work, I still expected to hear my phone ring at eleven-thirty when she would call me at lunch. But she wasn't in the kitchen waiting for me to come home to have dinner with her anymore. Her makeup mess no longer consumed the bathroom sink and her research papers and laptop were cleared from the dining table. She was gone, but she was everywhere. We were only in our early thirties. We were supposed to have forty or more years together.

My cousin, Mark, lived out west in a hole-in-the-wall town called Muerte in New Mexico. He called one day around three months after I had buried Morgan to tell me his neighbor, who owned the general store, was retiring and moving to be with his grandchildren so his house and the store were for sale. I was an accountant who had lived his whole life in the city. I had no idea how to run a convenience store in a small town. It felt like such a cliché but running away from my problems – from my memories – seemed like the best thing to do.

Mark handled almost everything and the old man flew to me to sign the final paperwork With tears in his eyes he shook my hand. Then he hugged me. He said he had raised two daughters and a son in that house and he'd opened that store forty-seven years ago. He was glad I was going to keep it going and Mark had assured him I would. He made me promise to take care of it all before moving on to finish out his life with his family.

I sent surprisingly few of my things ahead of me to New Mexico. As I touched each thing I packed, a memory from deep in the recesses of my brain moved forward. Most of them were once happy memories but now brought me pain. In the end, I took most of my clothes, a few family heirlooms, some photos, and a few other odd bits and things that I could stand. The rest was sold to an estate dealer.

As I flew to my new life, I watched the world change from

soulless cement buildings, to forest, to a patchwork quilt of agriculture, to mountains, and finally to desert. With the passage of hours and changing of scenery, I felt a change in myself. The sadness and melancholy that had consumed me those months gave way not to hope or excitement, but fear. I was fleeing everything I knew for a future I could not see.

Mark met me at the airport with a smile, a handshake, and a German Shepard who was more grey than black and tan. As we rode, Mark chattered on about how much I was going to love Muerte and how excited the town was to meet me. The store was a lynchpin to the community. It sold basic staples that people easily forgot and ran out of like cans of soup, toilet paper, pet food, and lighter fluid. The nearest supermarket was thirty-five minutes away.

"Most folks stock up there about once a month, get their little things at your store, produce from the farmer's market, and meat from Nelson's butchery. Your house is a few miles outside of the town hub but you got the company truck in the sale so you'll have something to get you places," he explained as we left civilization and headed into the sand and stone.

He forewarned me about a few of the residents. Mrs. Finnigan was an alcoholic in her seventies that liked to pinch men's bottoms and pretend she was innocent. The Lucas twins were seventeen years old and might give me problems but they're well known to Sherriff Iglesias. A man by the name of Harris was a recluse who lived, well, no one really knew where but he was stockpiling ammunition and canned goods for when the government comes to enslave us all in the name of communism.

"You don't seem phased by any of this," Mark commented.

"I'm from Manhattan," I reminded him. "Every third interaction of my day is with someone mentally unstable and every eighth is with someone who recently committed a crime."

"Good point."

He turned down a long, dirt drive and pulled up in front of a white, wood-siding house that was browned with dirt.

"Home sweet home!" Mark handed me a ring with about twenty or so keys. "I don't remember which ones he said go to what but you'll figure it out. Truck's parked around back. When you leave, if you turn left and go back the way we came, turn right at the intersection, go three miles, and turn left at the grey mailbox. That'll take you to my house. If you see goats, you went too far. Now, if you turn right out of here, that'll put you right on Main Street and take you straight into town. Turn left at the post office and your store is a little ways down on the right. Cell reception out here is sketchy at best so try not to get too lost."

I nodded and thanked him. He promised to check in on me the next day. I approached the house. I felt as if I was dreaming it all. The heavy ring of keys in my hand felt like such a foreign object that I almost dropped it. I sifted through the keys, examining one after the other until I found an old brass one with an "H" engraved on it. It fit. I held my breath as I pushed the door open.

The open space I stepped into was far bigger than my old apartment. To the left, the kitchen was large and open, separated from the rest of the space by a countertop. The dining and living room were capped with a high, vaulted, white ceiling with a skylight. The floor was real hardwood and in need of refinishing but everything else from the walls to the back and side of the cabinet was covered in faux wood paneling. Four doors (three bedrooms and bathroom) opened directly off the living room. The boxes I had sent ahead were arranged neatly in the middle of the main living space. There was a faint layer of dust and a few cobwebs, but it otherwise seemed in good shape. I went from room to room and opened the cabinets and closets. He'd left a few kitchen items, some books, and a taxidermized roadrunner. I ended up back in the living room and as I surveyed my surroundings, I was suddenly tired. I returned to the largest bedroom and found a blanket in the closet. I made myself a nest on the floor. Home.

The next morning, I found some towels in my boxes, some jeans, and a black T-shirt. The shower was comforting once I figured out that the hot and cold sides of the dial were only suggestions. Cleaned and refreshed, I debated between getting to know my new house and town or diving headlong into my new shop. I decided I would need the truck either way and wandered out to the back. The grass was broad and rough textured and mostly dead. The covered patio had a glass table and three mismatched chairs. Parked in the back part of the driveway was the work truck I had inherited.

I'm not sure what I was expecting. Maybe some nineteen-forties rust bucket or a box truck. Whatever I was expecting to have found, it was not the bright blue, barely two-year-old pickup that I found. I examined it. The outside was dusty just like everything else but there wasn't a single scratch, ding, or chip in that paint. I opened the door. I almost anticipated the new car smell to hit me. The upholstery and floor mats were pristine though a little sun-faded it seemed in places. I found the keys in the cupholder. Situating myself behind the wheel,

I turned the ignition and nothing happened. I tried again. Nothing.

I called Mark. "Hey, if you're nearby I could use a jump."

"Be right there."

Moments later, Mark and his German Shepard followed me out to the truck.

"Do you take that with you everywhere?" I indicated the dog.

"*That*," he said, "is my business partner and best friend."

"What about Kayla?"

"A wife is an entirely different animal."

I felt a twinge of sadness but said nothing. I needed to develop a thicker skin. Mark seemed to notice a shift in me because he promptly changed the subject.

"What's the truck doing?" he asked.

"Nothing."

"Nothing at all?"

"No."

"Huh. Well, I shouldn't be surprised. Never saw him drive the damn thing."

"What do you mean?"

"He never drove it. He bought it, used it for work once or twice for a month or so, then parked it back here and left it. Gas is probably bad too. Pop the hood."

I did as instructed and watched some kind of lizard scurry out of the engine bay and into the yard.

"At least those things don't bite. Probably about the only thing out here that won't try to kill ya."

I stared at him, trying to decide if he was being truthful or joking with me. He gave me a smile that really didn't answer.

He hooked a power pack to the battery terminals and talked about the lawn while it charged.

"Okay, give it a turn," he said.

I turned the key in the ignition. The engine emitted a whining, grinding noise. The dog pricked his ears and cocked his head at it. Mark fiddled with a few things under the hood and told me to try again. It had the same result, much to the consternation of the dog.

"Tell you what," he said. "We'll go into town to my garage and get some spark plugs, a gas can, and a few other things and get to work on this."

I, having never actually looked in the engine bay of a car before, knew I would be of no help at all and might actually be a hindrance.

"You mind dropping me at my store along the way so I can start sorting things out? That's where I was trying to go. I'll pay you for all this, of course, and no family discount, either."

"You got it."

The drive into town was about twelve minutes of very blank landscape with a few trees. Most of the buildings in town were built between the sixties and eighties and were fairly unremarkable. I knew they wouldn't be the old western-style saloons like you saw in the movies, but the little boy in me had been hopeful. The only traffic light in town was at the corner of Fifth and Main. As we waited for it to turn green, Mark told me about how there was almost a town riot over its installation. He then turned left at the post office and about half a mile down, pulled off to the side of the road and parked. I handed him one of the truck keys and put the other on my already-burdened ring.

"That's it." He pointed to a little brown building with white letters that said "MARKET" on it. "If you get hungry around lunchtime, Mrs. Boggs sells lunchmeat sandwiches at the butchery down on Third from eleven-thirty to one-thirty. I'll be back to get ya later."

I nodded, thanked him for everything, and exited the car. I stepped up to the front door and examined the worn, brass hardware. I then examined the ring of keys until I found a worn, round one with a similar patina. I slid it into the deadbolt, turned it, and heard it click. I was anxious and even shaking a little as I opened the door to *my* store.

I closed the door behind me and leaned against it as I surveyed the shop. Rows upon rows of four-foot-tall wooden bookshelves lay before me. They were stained a dark, deep, almost mahogany color and were obviously handmade decades ago. Items that needed to hang were on pegs on the walls to the left and right while fishing rods and ammunition were against the wall behind the long desk used as a checkout counter. I strolled down the rows of shelves. Canned goods, pet food, toilet paper, aspirin and cold remedies, cereal... all the nonperishable staples a person could want or need. There was not a speck of dust on any of the items, the wood shelves were properly oiled and the tile floor was polished to a high shine. The man had clearly taken a great deal of pride in the store and I realized why he had been so emotional when we had met. I suddenly felt a knot in the pit of my stomach as I realized the expectations I would have to live up to.

In the back of the shop, I found a small office space with a glass door and the basics in it; a desk, some shelves with binders, a filing cabinet, etc. took up most of the tiny workspace. There was also a minifridge with a microwave on top for lunches. I sat in the chair behind the desk and slowly spun around, taking in my surroundings. Where do I even begin? I supposed I should familiarize myself with the inventory. The man did run a successful business in a small town for nearly half a century so I would assume he knew what he should stock. I stopped spinning and looked at the desk. No computer. I went out and checked the counter. There was a push-button register, but no computer. There was also a very sad-looking goldfish in a bowl with a bubbler but no filtration. *Note to self, order an aquarium.*

I returned to the office and a green, spiral-bound notebook on the desk caught my eye. *Oh... oh, no...* I opened it to find pages and pages of handwritten ledgers, inventory logs, and more, much of which had been written in now-faded or smudged pencil. *I'm an accountant. I can figure this out.*

I spent hours making additional notes and corrections as I deciphered the ledgers. Periodically, I'd return to the shelves to check SKUs and barcodes. Around noon my stomach made an unholy sound and I realized that in my excited state, I hadn't had so much as a cup of coffee that morning. I returned to the shelves and found myself a bowl of microwave soup. I had debated finding my way to the butchery for a sandwich but the parade of people who had been peeking in the windows all morning trying to get a glimpse of the outsider already had me feeling a bit like an animal at the zoo. I returned to the back office and did my best to ignore them.

At 430 Mark and his Shepard pulled up out front. I shoved some staples like toilet paper, coffee, a few canned goods, and some soap in a box. I hopped in his car and sighed as I put my head against the headrest.

"How was your first day?" he asked.

"I felt like a freak on display. I think every person who walked by peeked in the windows at me."

"You're new. And to be fair, a lot of folks are relying on you to get the store back open so they don't have to make long trips out of town. 'Lot more are afraid you're going to change a lot of things. People in towns like this don't take well to change."

"First change I'm making is a computer system. His ledger system worked but by God, it must have been time-consuming."

Mark laughed. "He did a lot of that stuff in his head."

"How did people feel when you and Kayla moved here?"

"We got a lot of stares but she's born and bred in New Mexico so she fit in pretty quick. My Hoosier ass took a little more time. I remember I asked Ms. Baker for a double-dip ice cream cone and she looked at me like I had eight heads! Apparently, you're just supposed to say two scoops. But once I got my shop up and running and proved I was useful, they took to me. Just like they'll take to you once the initial stranger danger wears off."

I nodded. "I hope so." I thought for a moment. "Why did you and Kayla move here?"

"Well, you know we met in college." I nodded so he continued. "Well school just wasn't for me but she sure was. I agonized over how much I hated being a student but I wanted to make my parents proud. She encouraged me to talk to them and just be true to myself. I did. It went about as well as could be expected. A lot of yelling. But she always stood by me and supported my decisions no matter how broke I got. When she finished school, we weren't even talking marriage yet but when she said she wanted to come back down here to be closer to her family, it was a no-brainer. Settled in Muerte because we like the simple life, property was cheap, and we were both able to work."

"Do you ever regret it?"

"Sometimes. But for every downside, there are a dozen upsides." He pulled into my driveway. "Left your spare key in the glove box. She just needed a tune-up, fresh gas, and a little TLC but you're good to roll."

"You're amazing," I said as I got out of his car.

"I know."

"Send me the bill."

"Yeah, yeah." He waved his hand dismissively as he backed down onto the main street.

That night I feasted on canned ravioli while I set to making lists.

Home: 1. Bed 2. Sofa 3. Kitchen table and chairs 4. Dishes 5. Shower Curtain 6. Window curtains

Work: 1. Computer 2. Internet access 3. Blinds for office doors 4. Security cameras

I thought, plotted, and planned until I could barely keep my eyes open. I flipped off my lights and retreated to my nest on the floor.

Over the next several weeks, I made numerous trips into the city, loading the truck with various supplies and items. My first trip home saw the arrival of a mattress, box spring, and laptop computer for work. I ordered furniture and called to have services connected. All of the delivery and service trucks must have stirred something in the rumor mill because while I transcribed the ledgers of the last twelve months into my new inventory software, I sat in the office at the store. Even though I could not see the inquisitive stares through the newly hung blinds, I knew that they were there. When the new sign hung on the outside of the building, replacing the old "MARKET" sign with one that said "CARTER'S," a massive crowd formed on the sidewalk outside and it was several hours after dark before I could leave.

Eventually, I had set up the new laptop, familiarized myself with inventory, made connections with vendors, and installed a security system. Even the goldfish had a new twenty-gallon tank complete with a proper filtration system, a castle to hide in, and a new snail friend. I felt like I couldn't be any more prepared to open... theoretically, that is. In reality, I was terrified. I had uprooted my entire life, moved across the country, and sunk thousands of dollars into a business I didn't know how to run and a life I didn't know how to live. But there was no way to refrain from the inevitable and one sunny, spring morning, I breathed deep and flipped the sign on the front door to "OPEN" for the first time.

I hadn't even made it to the sales counter yet when I heard the doorbell ding. I turned to see an older woman, probably in her mid-seventies, with dyed red hair, blue eyelids, and matching blue fake pearls with the most unusually shaded pink lips I had ever seen.

"Good morning." I smiled at her.

"Who the Hell are you?" she asked indignantly.

"My name's Graham Carter. I'm the new proprietor here."

She looked at me from nose to toes. "What took you so long to open? John left everything pristine."

"He did," I agreed. "But I had to learn what he knew already. Make some changes and some upgrades."

"Changes and upgrades," she humphed. "If it's not broke, don't fix it." She turned and stomped down an aisle.

The door dinged again. A pretty blonde woman around my age came in and set a basket of lettuce, cabbage, and cucumbers on the counter.

"My name's Beth." She held out her hand.

I shook it. "Graham."

"Nice to meet you." She indicated the basket. "Welcome gift. I'll bring you by some corn and tomatoes when they are ready in the summer too. And if you're nice to me, I might even let you try some apples from my trees this fall."

I puffed up a little. "Thank you."

Before I could say anything else, the older woman shouted over the tops of the shelves. "This can't be right! John only charged a dollar forty-nine for toilet paper. This is marked at a dollar NINETY-nine!"

"Yes, ma'am." I tried to keep the smile on my face. "Changes and upgrades, like I told you earlier."

"Outrageous!"

Beth giggled. "Don't worry about Joyce. She'll be pinching your butt in no time."

A light blinked on in my head. "Ah! So that's Mrs. Finnigan!"

On cue, she threw the toilet paper on the counter. "Who told you my name?" she demanded.

"My cousin Mark, ma'am. He told me about a lot of the people here so I – uh – wouldn't feel so much like an outsider."

"Mark? Mark who?"

"Mauer. He owns the auto repair shop."

Her eyes narrowed. Then, in a blink, her entire demeanor changed. "Oh!" she fluttered. "Mark is your cousin?"

"Yes, ma'am. He's the reason I moved here."

"Well then." She picked up the toilet paper. "Welcome, Mr. Carter." She slid three one-dollar bills across the counter. "Keep the change." She had an extra sashay to her step as she left.

Beth cackled as I watched her leave, bewildered by the entire interaction. As she was walking out, a little girl around nine years old with dark hair and tan skin came in.

"I'm Esperanza!" she announced. "Everyone calls me Za."

"Hello, Za. I'm Mr. Carter."

"Nice to meet you." She shook my hand enthusiastically.

"What can I help you with today?"

"How much puppy food can I get for Chuy with this?"

She emptied her pockets of crumpled-up bills and loose change.

I counted it out. "Looks like a ten-pound bag and you'll have eight cents left."

"Grand!" her eyes lit up. "Where is it?"

I handed her the eight cents back. "Bottom shelf over there." I pointed.

I put her money with the three dollars into the till. She walked out of the front door carrying the bag.

"Thank you, Mr. Carter!" she called. "I'll be back when I have more money!"

"I wonder what she's feeding." Beth looked perplexed. "Her parents don't believe in pets. Animals have to either work or be eaten. I hope she's not hiding a dog somewhere."

"She seems like a good kid," I assessed.

"She is. But she's a lonely kid." Beth shook her head. "She was in my class last year. The other kids don't really interact with her and she plays by herself a lot. She tells a lot of stories but they're usually harmless. Honestly, I wouldn't be surprised if the dog is imaginary."

"Oh, you're a teacher?"

"Yes. Kayla teaches first grade and I teach fourth. She told me you were coming and that you may need some kindness from a local."

I felt my cheeks flush a little and three more customers came in. Beth smiled a pearly smile and excused herself.

The rest of the day went much the same way. Half the people were welcoming, inviting, and eager to share gossip. The other half were wary and distrustful. Many were upset about the increase in prices. A pair of identical teenagers came in and I made a point to mention the new cameras. They left quickly without purchasing anything. At five o'clock I locked the front door and turned to see Mark leaning against his car with the dog in the back seat.

"How was the first day?" he asked cheerfully.

"I survived," I said.

He laughed. "Come on. Kayla wants you to dinner."

I followed him past my house and on to his. He and Kayla shared a small, three-bedroom manufactured home from the sixties. The ceilings were a little low and the toilet ran, but it was cozy. Mark and I stood in the backyard each with a beer while he tended the grill.

I looked out over the horizon. The sun was setting in a brilliant display of orange and red.

"The sky is so different here," I said.

"It's the same sky," he said as he clicked his tongs. "It's just that here you can actually see it."

"You know," I continued. "I think this is the first real cookout I've ever been to."

He laughed a deep, hearty, belly laugh. "Cookout? This is just dinner. Wait until Fourth of July hits."

The next day went much the same way as the first. So did the next day. And the next. After the first two weeks, the town had finally accepted my existence. There were still a few who were upset about some of the changes I had made but most fell into a routine.

Once a week, Beth would come with produce from her property, sandwiches for us to have lunch, or a coffee in the morning. We'd spend an hour or so sharing stories or sometimes she would help me put inventory away. I really enjoyed her company. She made me feel welcome not only to the town but as a human being. Her smile lit up the shop and her laugh raised my heart. After she would leave, however, I would feel the unmistakable burden of guilt. Morgan was gone and I knew she would want me to be happy but I felt so unfaithful when I was with Beth. But she was like a drug. I looked forward to being around her every week and missed her when I was in the store alone.

The man known as Harris was the hardest to win over. He absolutely did not trust me and I had a feeling he believed

I was secretly working for the government though he never said so. He would come on Tuesdays and buy three boxes of ammunition and seventeen cans of food. Out of curiosity one day I asked him about the specific numbers of his items. He said anything more than that would alert the feds to his activities and now that I had a computer that transmitted everything to them, he would have to be extra careful. Just to toy with him, I pointed out that buying the exact same number of the exact same thing on the same day of every week created a pattern for them to find. He looked horrified just before he left. After that, he still always bought exactly twenty items but he would switch the quantities around a bit. It was still always on Tuesdays, though. He seemed a bit more trusting after I'd "helped him hide from the feds" more effectively.

On Mondays, Za would come in with the money she had earned over the weekend doing odd jobs for people around the town. She would buy the biggest bag of dog food she could afford and regale me with stories of how she had taught Chuy to come when called, sit, and play fetch. Once, I asked her if she would bring him by for me to see all the wonderful things she had taught him. She instantly became bashful and said that Chuy didn't like to be around people or strangers. I felt that confirmed the idea that her puppy wasn't real. After a while, I stopped seeing her so often and then I only saw her when she was on an errand for her parents. I assumed she had grown bored with her imaginary dog and stopped wasting her money on food for it. One day, her mother sent her for ibuprofen but the girl seemed particularly troubled.

"What's wrong, little one?" I asked.

She sighed as if she held the world above her head. "Our

chickens, Mr. Carter. They are disappearing and my Daddy is going to shoot whatever is doing it. He's just a hungry animal. It's not fair."

"I'm sorry, Za." I hugged her. "Maybe it'll move on to hunt somewhere else."

"Maybe." She sounded unconvinced.

Mrs. Finnigan also came on Mondays. She had taken a shine to me after she found out that I was related to the "handsome mechanic" and it was such a shame he was married. She also made mention of how it was so unfortunate I was a widower at such a young age but she'd be happy to provide me with whatever comfort I may need. Mark spit beer out of his nose when I told him about that conversation. I made sure to always stay behind the counter when she was in the store or at the very least, kept my butt out of her arm's reach.

The Fourth of July celebration was everything Mark had claimed. I had been in town for over 2 months and learned most of the people's purchasing habits. I ordered in some sparklers, pennants, flags, and red, white, and blue disposable plates and cups. I sold out of everything in less than two days. Mark and Kayla had me and Beth over for dinner so we could watch the fireworks from their backyard. The women fussed over side dishes and setting the picnic table while Mark manned the grill with steaks, potatoes, and ears of corn. I, having lived most of my life on microwavable food or takeout, successfully tossed the salad and made a pretty presentable centerpiece from a few flags and ribbon.

"Hey, you know the Gonzales farm up the road?" Mark asked as he handed me a cold bottle of beer.

"The one with the goats?"

"Not anymore." He shook his head.

"What happened?"

"Total mystery. First, the Martins lose their chickens. Then the Gonzales place loses one goat, then another, then four in one night. Then, poof, the whole herd is gone."

I knew nothing about goats or farming but tried not to sound like a complete novice. "Coyotes?" I asked.

"Damndest thing. Coyotes leave bodies and blood. But here, there ain't nothing left. Not a trace of the animals or prints from the predator. It's like they just vanished into the breeze or something."

We mulled it over a bit before the topic changed to work. Beth joined us and brought a big bowl of potato salad and a plate of deviled eggs. I helped her arrange them on the table. Kayla brought a pitcher of spiked, ice-cold lemonade and kissed her husband. Seeing them happy together made me miss Morgan but I looked at Beth out of the corner of my eye and I knew that kind of happiness could be possible again.

We ate, drank, and laughed. When I thought the food was gone, Kayla appeared with a chocolate cake and somehow, I made room in my too-full stomach. After dark, the sky lit up with explosions of color. Beth and I sat on the same bench of the picnic table, leaning against each other. I felt my fingers lift as she slid her hand under mine. I looked her in the eye. She smiled that magical smile and I couldn't deny the spell she had cast on me. I closed my fingers around her hand and we watched the brilliant sky.

For the next month or so everything seemed like routine but I began to notice a few odd things. Harris stopped coming in for his weekly collection of canned goods and bullets. Mrs. Gonzales didn't come by for cereal for the kids and even Mrs. Finnigan wasn't coming in anymore.

One sunny, fall Tuesday, Sherriff Iglesias stopped in. "Morning, Graham."

"Morning, Eric. What can I do for you?"

"You mind if I put up a few of these posters?"

He handed me a sheet of paper. There was a picture of a little girl in a flower printed sundress. She had puffy cheeks that hid her eyes when she smiled. It read: MISSING. ANNABELLE GRANGER. TEN YEARS OLD. LAST SEEN AT MUERTE MUNICIPAL PUBLIC PARK ON AUGUST 20TH.

"Of course, I don't mind! That's terrible!"

"I know," he lowered his eyes. "I have no leads at all. You haven't heard anything in the rumor mill, have you? I know folks like to gossip when they come in here."

"I haven't." I shook my head. "But I have noticed something odd."

"Like what?"

I told him about the recent disappearances of my regular customers.

"That is very disheartening. People of this town are creatures of habit. Can't check on Harris on account that no one actually knows where he lives. He has a box at the post office and he gets his mail on Tuesdays. I'll check and see if they've seen him recently. I knew about Mrs. Gonzales. Her husband told a friend who is cousins with my secretary that they had gotten in a fight and he thought she left to go to her sister's house and cool off. But Joyce? That old bat could be dead on her bathroom floor and no one would notice. I'll look into it."

As he left, Beth walked in and saw the poster. "Oh, no. They still haven't found her?"

I shook my head. "Did you know her?"

"She was in my class last year. You know what else? The Lucas twins went missing a week ago, too."

It turned out I was right. Mrs. Gonzales, Mrs. Finnigan, Harris (as far as we could tell), Annabelle, and the Lucas twins had all vanished without a trace. No evidence was left behind anywhere. Mrs. Finnigan's house was immaculate with no signs of struggle. No one had seen anything at the park when Annabelle had gone missing, and the twins were known to camp in the desert outside of town so it had been a while before anyone noticed they were missing. All of their things were found at their campsite as if they had just randomly decided to walk off into oblivion.

One night, as I was locking up the shop, I turned and saw a silhouette across the street. Esperanza stood looking out over the sunset. She tucked her thumbs into the front pockets of her denim jeans. Her long, dark hair hung over her shoulders like a curtain that gently blew in the breeze. Her posture and stance exuded sadness and maybe a little loneliness.

"What's wrong little one?" I asked.

She turned to me. Her eyes were red and tear-stained.

"Chuy." She sniffed. "He's sick."

"Will your parents take him to the vet?" I knew he was an imaginary puppy, but if she had been my daughter, I would have found a way to play along.

"No. They don't believe he is real and they don't approve of pets either."

"Well, maybe I can help."

Her eyes brightened and she stood a little straighter. "Really, Mr. Carter? Would you do that?"

"Of course, Za. But you told me he doesn't like people. Are you sure he will be okay to see me?"

"Oh, yes! I'm sure he will be very happy to see you!"

"Okay then." I opened the truck door. "Take me to the patient and I'll see what I can do."

She eagerly climbed into the passenger seat of my truck and we rode out into the dusty countryside. Ten or so minutes into the desert, she pointed to a rock formation.

"Left there, Mr. Carter."

The light was fading but I could just make out a narrow bend that led into the rocks.

"You come all the way out here by yourself?"

She giggled. "I'm not by myself. I have Chuy to protect me. Stop here."

I parked the truck and she eagerly leaped out.

"Chuy? Chuy?" she called.

I smiled and expected her to run forward and return to me with a bundle in her arms that only a child's imagination could see. But no. In the darkness, I saw a great, hulking shape rise from a crevice in the rocks. It was a bear. *No, not a bear.* It stood like a bear but had no fur to speak of. Bare skin was stretched over a lean frame, prominently showing every muscle bundle. The head was narrow and the ears were pointed much like a dog's. The eyes were black and glassy and glinted in the dimming light. At the end of each digit of its five-toed paws were four-inch claws. It stood upright and must have been eight feet tall.

"Esperanza!" I yelled and ran for her; afraid the thing would devour her whole.

I tripped and fell in the dirt. I looked up and she was still standing with the... thing.

"It's okay, Mr. Carter. Chuy won't hurt me."

"Esperanza. That is not a dog." My voice came as a mild squeak. My heart was caught in my throat and it choked my speech.

"Silly. I never said he was a dog. I fed him puppy food when he was little." She was standing next to the thing and patting its back as it sat down on its haunches. "Then he needed more meat so I fed him our family's chickens. Then goats because he got big and we ran out of chickens. He really liked the goats. I think that's what he's supposed to eat."

Goats? Chuy? My head spun. "Is... is he a chupacabra?" I asked her, barely believing the words that were coming out of my mouth.

"Of course!" She was so matter-of-fact and virtually nonchalant.

"Those are a myth," I argued.

She laughed. "Does he *look* like a myth? Anyway, when Mr. Gonzalez ran out of goats, Chuy started hunting for his own food. I was afraid he would get caught so I started bringing it to him."

I finally took my eyes off the monster before me and my gaze met hers. There I saw a different monster. Her face no longer belonged to the innocent little girl who would come into my shop. It was hardened and menacing. The eyes were devoid of any compassion. I didn't recognize her at all.

"Esperanza?" I asked cautiously.

"After he ate the crazy man with all the guns, I couldn't risk letting him be found. I showed him where those mean boys were camping and let him help himself. The old lady was always sticking her nose where it didn't belong so it was her fault she followed me out here. I do feel kind of bad about Annabelle. She was always nice to me. I'm sorry, Mr. Carter. I really like you. But Chuy is the only real friend I have ever had."

"I'm your friend!" I protested.

"I know. I'm sorry. But Chuy is my BEST friend." She said this with no remorse at all.

"Za..."

She shook her head. "Supper!"

It lunged, propelling itself forward with powerful back legs. I scrambled to my feet and ran. I ducked between two large rocks and into a crevice it could not squeeze through. I sidled through the gap as it struggled to get up and over the rocks. I circled around the formation and fell into a pile of bones and clothing that had been bleached from baking in the sun. All those missing people. This wasn't real. This was a dream. I'm in a horror movie. Running from monsters and tripping on bones aren't things that happen in real life. A sound somewhere between a scream and a growl pierced the darkness and reminded me that this was definitely real. It sounded to my left. I ran right, recognized part of the cliff face, and turned right again. There was my truck. I jumped in and slammed the door behind me. The cab knocked sideways as the creature hit it with all its force. It clawed at the door panel and my hand shook as I frantically reached for the keys. No keys.

I looked forward and Esperanza stood in front of the truck, dangling the keys from her finger. Not knowing what to do, I leaned on the horn. The noise startled the creature and it jumped back. It looked at me with its head cocked the way Mark's German Shepard had done. Mark. The key. I opened the glove box and the spare truck key sat on top of a stack of papers. I put it in the ignition and turned it. The side window shattered and I'm not sure if the scream I heard was from me or the creature. I threw the truck in reverse and hit the gas as hard as I could. I saw it run towards me and could hear Esperanza yell something as I swung the truck, fearing for a split second it might flip over. I switched to drive and drove very literally for my life. I struggled to keep the steering wheel steady as my hands shook uncontrollably.

I looked at my cell phone. No reception. When I'd get back, I would immediately call... Who? The police? Esperanza's parents? They wouldn't care that she was in the desert alone and if I told Sherriff Iglesias there was an eight-foot-tall monster in the desert being fed people by a little girl, he'd lock me away. I could at least tell him I found the bones. But then the creature – the CHUPACABRA – would kill him too. What could I do? Who could I tell? Beth and Mark wouldn't believe me. Even *I* wouldn't believe me. No one would.

When I finally got home, I bolted the door and checked all of the windows. For days I was too afraid to sleep, passing out occasionally from pure exhaustion. Every bird outside my window and mouse inside my wall was Chuy coming to finish what he had started. Mark called to check in on me when the store hadn't opened in three days. I told him I was very sick and couldn't leave the house. Beth stopped by with a care package but I couldn't let her in. I didn't know what I would say to her. I told her I was contagious and promised to see her when I was better. She was a little crestfallen but said she understood and left the thermos of homemade soup and orange juice on the porch. When I opened the door to retrieve it, I found something else. My key ring, the one Esperanza had taken from me that night, was laying on my welcome mat.

It was nine days before I ran out of food and pulled myself together enough to leave my house. I parked my truck in front of CARTER'S and a group of people began to swarm me, expressing joy that I was better and assuring me that they had prayed for me and that I had been missed. Beyond the crowd I could see her and my heart dropped to the bottom of my stomach when our eyes locked.

Esperanza stood on the sidewalk. She smiled at me and held her index finger to her lips.

That was the last time I ever saw her. Three days later, Sheriff Iglesias came by with another missing poster for the bulletin board. Za's eyes, cold and black, looked at me from an unsmiling black and white photo. Eventually, I got up the nerve to tell the sheriff where the bones were. I lied and told him I found them while out on a hike. I could at least give the families, all except Esperanza's, a little peace of mind. I don't know if she was eaten or if she ran away with her pet. But she was the last resident of Muerte, New Mexico to disappear and I knew that the monster had moved on.

14

Twinkle Sparkle

Twinkle, sparkle
Little star
Way up in
Heaven afar.
Cast your light
And let me peek.
No discerning
Strong or weak.
Night by night
I watch you shine
And pretend
That you are mine.
Shine bright
Little light.
Streak across the sky.
Falling falling.

No time to cry.
Then I wish
Upon my star
Together forever
Until we die.

15

Forgive Yourself

A trick of mind
be-stills the heart
and renders the body
impaired.

To tell oneself
you're not as brave
and convinced you can't be
repaired.

You are your own
antagonist
in this story of your
being.

To be yourself

you must be kind,
absolve your psyche; soul
freeing.

16

End of Days

    I had a dream
That I was a queen
And looked down upon my land

'Twas peaceful still
As the farmers till
And families lend an hand

But in the air
I saw warning there
As the angels took their leave

There would be war
And tranquil no more
As the earth could no more breathe

Crops were to fail
And pestilence to prevail
As all life began to choke

What have we done
The devil has won
As greed his wrath did provoke

It is the end
Of my reign, my friend
My shrine to say "Mother Earth"

17

Nothing Rhymes with Orange

Disclosure: it was late and I'd had a bit of pinot grigio when I wrote this.

Red
Moon's halo
Soft tulip bed

Yellow
Dandelion
Blooms so mellow

Green
Peacocks
Feathers to preen

Blue
Of your
Love's gaze at you

Indigo
Gemstones
And potter's throw

Violet
Twilight
Falling stars set

18

Brick by Brick

Brick by brick I pull myself along the walkway in front of the little white house. My mangled legs dragging uselessly behind me leave a snail-trail of blood along the ground.

If she discovers I'm still alive... Brick by brick I keep pulling.

I don't know where I'm going but I cannot stay here.

If she finds me... Brick by brick.

I've made it this far. If I can make it to the road maybe someone will find me and help me. Brick by brick.

But I see her cherry-red convertible turn from the road and into the driveway. I freeze. Do I scream? Maybe a neighbor will hear me. I hear her stilettos clicking against the walkway as she approaches me brick by brick.

19

Fortune Teller

White daisy petals
Please do not lie.
Will he love me
Before I die?

Pluck: he loves me.
Pluck: he does not.
He kisses me
Without a thought.

Is this true love?
Maybe farewell?
My heart may break
If you don't tell.

Pluck one is yes.
Pluck two is no.
Pluck five, perhaps.
Five more to go.

His eyes so soft.
His hands so strong.
Words so distant.
Alone so long.

Pluck six is nay.
Pluck ten is too.
This can't be right.
I do love you.

20

Side by Side

My Dearest Elizabeth,

I feel silly, yet compelled to write to you. I am you at the age of thirty-five. I am writing this letter because I wish someone had told me what I am going to tell you.

Directly following college, at the age of twenty-two, you are going to be working for a plump and balding man named Dr. Greensburg. He will insist you call him Ralph, but you will maintain your professional distance. Everything that you have worked hard for will seemingly have fallen into place. You will have your own apartment with a balcony that overlooks the river. Mom is only a ten-minute drive away so you can have Sunday dinners together. While you have mounds of debt on the back of your mind, your late nights of caffeine-fueled frenzied studying are over and you will have a relaxing job that makes you happy.

Yet, through all of this, you will have a hollow part of your soul. You will get a cat named Ebony and she will fill some of the void, but it will still be there. Every day you will feel it getting bigger and more consuming. You won't know what is missing. The pit will be there like a sinkhole that gradually opens wider and sucks your happiness in. You will go through your days with a smile and pretend that everything is well. You will lie to Mom about it. But, when you are home alone with your cat, it will consume you.

Then, one day, the universe will send you Austin. He will bring his niece in for an upset stomach. The attraction will be powerful and instant. He was tall and muscular. His eyes were an ocean blue and were so soulful, they will pull you in. He will take his hat off to show a messy mop of chestnut hair. When he shakes your hand to introduce himself, it will completely engulf yours. The warmth from such a simple act will cut straight through to your heart and you will find it hard to breathe. After his niece's exam, you will go over discharge instructions with him. Afterward, he is going to ask you to coffee.

I remember how it felt. There are rules about dating a patient. But he wasn't a patient. The pain from the breakup with Ryan at the beginning of college was still very real. Being fresh out of school and trying to find that place of belonging in the world made it feel like a terrible time to start dating. You must ignore all doubts and take a leap of faith. Austin was not Ryan. There is no niche that you will fit perfectly into. You will need to find what makes you happy and I promise Austin will do that.

Coffee that Sunday afternoon was perfect. His smile lit up the whole room and those blue eyes focused on me made me feel like I was the only person in the café. He loved that I am a nurse and devote my life to helping people. He talked at length about baseball though, eventually realizing he was hogging the conversation, he returned the conversation to me. The walk in the park after coffee was even more magical. He was an amateur entomologist and spent hours turning over leaves and rocks to expose and explain the bugs he found. Despite the abnormality of the topic, his enthusiasm was contagious. After wandering back to the cars, the kiss goodbye was truly pure. For the first time in a long time, I had good butterflies in my stomach.

That will be the beginning of almost ten years of happiness. It will start with just weekends together and hours upon hours on the phone after work every night. You will go camping together, see Ireland together, and talk about starting a family. Every night he told me he would love me until our bodies lay side-by-side in the ground. That consuming void inside you will finally be filled.

When Mom dies, you will feel like you have no one left. That void will start growing back again. Your days will seem bleak and dark. You will not want to wake up in the morning, but you won't be able to sleep either. But Austin will be there. He will hold you while you cry. He will make sure you eat and take care of Ebony when you can't. He will steadily stitch that hole in your heart back together.

But as the years go on, you will become distant. You will go to work for a major hospital that forces you to keep odd hours and he will start to travel more for work. You will see less and less of each other and when you are together, you will argue about how little time you spend together. The fights will become aggressive. Pillows will be thrown. Plates will be broken. Doors will be slammed.

Eventually, he will tell you he wants it to end.

The tears in his eyes when he said it were like daggers that pierced through to my core. My life flowed out through those wounds and that void grew bigger than it ever had been before. When he turns to walk away, out the kitchen door -- and out of your life -- you will grab him by the shirt and try to stop him. He will lose his balance and crack his head on the corner of the kitchen counter.

There is so much blood.

You may be wondering why I am telling you all of this. It is because I want you to know that you will find happiness. You will be fulfilled, but, I'm sorry to say that you will not get that family you dreamed of. You will not live to see thirty-six.

I cannot imagine my life without him. I don't want the void to return. I must end this letter now. I have selected a knife from a block on the very counter he hit his head. I must fulfill my promise and love him until our bodies are side by side.

21

Condemn my Soul

I have no words. What once came to me with great ease and finesse has not escaped me entirely. My heart beats in my throat and I try to force myself to blink. Here she stands before me. To call her Aphrodite would be an insult. The goddess herself cannot hold a candle to the beauty my eyes behold. I want so much to reach out and touch her. To feel her against my fingertips and know that she is real, that this is not just some dream my subconscious has conjured to torment me. But I cannot. She is a treasure behind glass at a museum. I can look at her, appreciate her, even worship her to my heart's desire. But I will never have her. She belongs to another. I would give the last twenty years of my life to be him if it would give me twenty days to call her mine. Envy may be a sin, but so is lust and I would gladly condemn my soul for her.

22

Free write Aug 20, 2023

There I lay in the dark in a cold bed that wasn't mine. Through the open window I could hear traffic and a dog barking down below. Somewhere in the distance, a train blew its whistle in the night. Inside the room, the only sound was a soft, droning snore from the man I was sharing a bed with.

He lay on his side while I lay on mine with a great void between us. While what had just transpired between us had been raw and passionate, I knew the only love that could cross that chasm in the bed came from me. He knew how I felt about him. He did not reciprocate and while I respected that, it was still an open wound.

23

Stand and Fall

Here I stand
Alone
Braced against the odds
Barren and exposed
Here I lay
I weep
With no one to catch my tears
For all my struggles
For all my faith
No one is here
I stand alone
No love
All lost
This lie
Called life
Has left me hollow

I will stand
again
Waiting to
Fall again

24

Sabine

On Facebook, I asked my followers to provide me with a noun, a verb, and an adjective to inspire one of my short stories. A follower provided me with the following: Catnip, Flummox, and Labyrinthine. As provided by her inspiration I now present to you "Sabine."

"You're sure this is what you want?" I feel myself choke as I say it.

She nods. "Yes," she whispers softly as her cornflower blue eyes fill with tears.

"This is NOT what I want," I say more sternly, steeling myself.

"I know." One of the tears escapes her eye and rolls down her right cheek.

"I don't want to live without you. What about our plans to retire to Greece? We were supposed to have fifty or more years from when I put that ring on your finger."

"I'm sorry." She looks down at her hands in her lap.

Eleven years together. Eleven. And she is choosing to end it all as if our vows had meant nothing. I focus on keeping the rage that is boiling in me suppressed. I do not want what will likely be our last conversation to be a fight.

Eleven years ago I had been a fledgling anthropology major. It was the first day of classes. I was rushing hastily across campus with my bag bouncing against my back. It was hot out for early fall but I felt a sudden jolt and my belly felt like it was on fire.

"Oh, my God!" A female voice exclaimed. "Oh, my God. Are you okay?"

My brain, lagging from lack of sleep due to anxiety about the day, suddenly kicked in to piece together what had just happened. A pretty redhead was scrambling to pick up some notebooks from the ground with one hand while holding an empty travel mug that was missing the lid in the other. I looked down at myself. My grey Nirvana band shirt was soaked through. I had collided with this girl but how had I not seen her?

Then she stood and looked UP at me. WAY up.

I had been six-foot-one since my sophomore year of high school. I was used to being taller than the people around me but there in front of me was the shortest girl I had seen on campus. She was a leprechaun with a sweet, round face and black plastic glasses that framed amazingly blue eyes that captivated me completely. Her long red hair was pulled up into a ponytail on top of her head with a black scrunchie and the top of her black t-shirt was as wet as my shirt.

"I'm so sorry. Are you okay?" she asked again.

"Am I okay?" I was a little dumb-struck by the question and more awestruck by her beauty.

"Yeah," she said, looking at me with a quizzical expression on her face. "My tea was really hot."

I looked back at my wet shirt. The scalded skin underneath was tender and probably pink, but I wasn't going to let her know that.

"I'll live. Are you okay? I might as well have been a steamroller running over you. I'm really sorry about that."

"It's okay." She smiled. Two of her bottom teeth were just slightly crooked and I couldn't help but find it endearing.

"When you have to live in boots just to be five feet tall, you get kind of used to it." She indicated the black leather footwear with one-inch heels that was partially hidden by her jeans.

"Uh—" *Come on, brain. Say something.*

No. I just looked down at her, slack-jawed like a monkey with a jigsaw puzzle and unsure of what to say. I had never interacted very much with girls in high school and at that moment, my anxiety was in overdrive.

"Are you sure you're okay?" she asked warily.

I nodded. "Yeah, I'm just not thinking clearly for some reason."

She smiled that sweet, adorable smile. "Well, I'd better get to class. I'm sorry, again."

She put her hand on my arm. I think, in that moment, I knew what it felt like to stick a fork in a light socket. All of my hair stood at attention and my heart started desperately trying to break free of my ribcage.

"Oh. Right," I sputtered. "Maybe I'll see you around..." I trailed off.

"Sabine." She pronounced it Za-bee-nuh and I felt my smile grow as I heard each syllable.

I spent the rest of my day (no exaggeration) replaying our interaction in my head. There were a million and two things I could have and should have said. *Would you like to have lunch? Can I buy you another tea? Hi, my name's Nash.* A few times between classes I thought I saw her but I was a little afraid to approach her in case my brain decided I was on my own again.

That evening, I sat at my desk in my room while my mother made dinner downstairs. I was finding it very hard to concentrate on my schoolwork not because Sabine was running through my head (she was, but that wasn't why) but because Consuela, my normally standoffish calico cat, kept rubbing up against me, trying to climb in my lap, and licking my shirt until it was wet again. Finally, I had to lock her out of my bedroom. After dinner, when I had showered and returned to my room, I found her curled up in the t-shirt on the floor next to the hamper. What was going on with her and that shirt?

The next morning, I actually ran a comb through my hair and put on a blue checkered button-down shirt over a clean white t-shirt. I knew I was doing it on the off chance I would run into Sabine (not literally this time) but I was hoping she wouldn't figure that out. I took a long, hard look in the mirror. Satisfied that I looked clean without looking like I'd put in too much effort, I went downstairs to breakfast.

Keenan, my older brother by a whopping sixteen minutes,

whistled as he sat at the table. "Who are you all dressed up for?"

"No one. What are you talking about? Shut up," I said anxiously as I put two pop-tarts in the toaster and poured myself a cup of coffee.

"Right." He nodded and smiled. "What's her name?"

"I don't know what you're talking about."

The toaster sprang and startled me so much that the lid on the mug was the only thing that saved me from my second scalding in as many days.

"So jumpy. Is it because of that cute little redhead you tried to mow over yesterday?"

I bit my lips together. He grinned.

"You saw that?" I asked.

"Dude, pretty much the whole school was out there before classes. I bet at least half of them saw it. What they probably didn't notice that I did was you doing that thing where you crack your knuckles over and over when you're nervous. Oh, and the look of sheer panic on your face. I'm sure she just figured you're shy. Or dumb. She's right either way." He shrugged.

I stuffed my pop-tart in my mouth and looked at the floor in shame. Keenan and I were both tall with dark hair and brown eyes but that was as far as our twin similarities extended. He had a large nose – a schnoz, if you will – that came to a point, harkening back to our Greek heritage where mine was round and more button-like. Also like our Greek ancestry, he took great pride in physical prowess. He was at the gym four days a week, watched his diet carefully, and had a perpetual tan from outdoor summer activities. He was a lifeguard, quarterback, shortstop, and ran track. He was friends with everyone and had a girlfriend (though rarely the same girl for long) consistently since we had been in the sixth grade.

I, on the other hand, preferred video games, listening to music and hanging out with the same two friends I'd had since kindergarten, and reading. I wasn't pasty, but I was maybe a little pale. I wasn't fat, but there was just a bit of fleshy overlap over my belt. I hated sports, new things gave me anxiety, and I'd dated enough girls to count on one hand. Keenan outshined me in almost every aspect of our lives but I was mostly content to live in his shadow. How we were twins was a question I'd asked as many times as there are stars in the sky.

Keenan clapped me on the shoulder. "Talk to her, man. Come on, we have to go to class."

We got on our bikes and rode the just under four miles to campus. Freshmen weren't allowed to have cars, which I felt was a stupid rule. We locked our bikes in the rack alongside the others and he headed off to join his friends.

"Talk to her!" he called over his shoulder.

I removed my coffee from the holder that was meant for water bottles. I unlocked the lid and drank deeply. Talk to her. Easy for Mr. Perfect to say. If we were identical twins maybe he could take my place to break the ice and test to see if she would even be interested in a date. But, no. We shared a womb but not DNA. *Just talk to her? Dude, you saw my brain shut down yesterday.*

And then, there she was. Her hair was tied up in the same ponytail and she wore the same slender black boots. Her blue shirt was just a few shades darker than her eyes. She was standing with a group of other girls and they were all smiling. Why did they have to travel in flocks? It made it so hard to talk to just one of them. The others would swarm around her and protect her and ask a million questions if I just tried to say hello. Okay, I guess I understand why they did it but it really make things hard for guys like me. I still wasn't sure what I was going to say to her and contemplated backing away slowly, but she made the decision for me.

She glanced away from the group and her eyes caught mine. She smiled, said something to the others, and started to walk in my direction. My heart either stopped or sped up so fast I couldn't tell it was beating at all. I'm really not sure which. I heard Keenan's voice in my head. *Just talk to her. I'm called Nash. What the eff was that? Your eyes are really blue. Yes, let's go the serial killer route. Come on, man, she's getting closer. Come so I can ruin your tea, again? The tea.*

I looked and saw the same cup (with the lid) in her left hand. My shirt. My cat.

"Hi," she said, stopping a few feet from me.

"Hi," I said back. I wanted to sound calm. I did NOT sound calm.

"You looked like you had something you wanted to say to me."

"I uh—" *Come ON, MAN. What is wrong with you?* "I was wondering what was in that tea. Connie was all over me last night."

"Connie?" she knitted her eyebrows and took a step back.

"Cat!" I blurted out. "Consuela is my cat." I tried to reign myself in.

Her face softened and she gave a little giggle. "That's probably because it's catnip tea."

"Catnip?"

She pulled the lid off her mug and held it up for me to smell. "Yeah, it's used for anxiety and nervousness and a few other things."

"Anxiety? I may have to try that."

She smiled as she put the lid back on her cup. "Is that all you wanted to ask me? About my tea?"

"Well, I. Um. Also wanted to know if I could maybe take you out for a tea sometime? I owe you for the one I spilled."

"Do you even drink tea?" There was an air of skepticism in her voice.

"No. Coffee." I held up my mug.

She giggled a little and looked me up and down. "On one condition."

"What's that?" I held my breath.

"You tell me what your name is."

I exhaled a little louder than I meant to. "Nash. My name is Nash Huxley."

"Huxley? Like Keenan Huxley?"

Of course, you know my brother. Everybody does. I tried to smile. "Yeah, we're twins."

"Really?" she scanned my face, looking for a resemblance.

"I look like Dad. He looks like mom."

"I have a few classes with him. Are you the showy, popular, athletic type too?"

"No, I'm the hide in my room or have a panic attack in crowds type." *Why did I say that out loud?*

Her already bright eyes lit up. "Good. That's more my

type." She opened her notebook, scribbled something on a piece of paper, ripped off the corner, and stuffed it in my hand. "Call me after 6 p.m."

Her eyes were so blue and bright then. They held me captive not only through our first date but for the next eleven years of our lives together. But not now. Now they are sunken and dull. They are rimmed with red because she has been crying. She is choosing to end eleven years of mostly happiness and break my heart.

I remember watching her walk down the aisle five years after we met. I knew my mom was crying in the front row. I knew Keenan was standing next to me, tall and proud in his tux. I knew the pianist was playing somewhere in the back of the crowd. But I could only see her and all the world was silent. She was a vision in white lace with white daisies tucked in her flowing red hair. No veil to hide her beauty, only flowers to make her more surreal. She held a bundle of the same daisies in front of her as she came towards me. Our eyes locked and she smiled. I couldn't breathe.

Her father placed her hand in mine. "You take care of my little girl," he said.

"I will," I promised.

A single tear escaped Sabine's right eye as she kissed her father's cheek before he took his seat.

Was the officiant talking? I didn't hear a thing. I had no idea what was going on until Keenan stuck his finger in my ear to snap me out of my trance and hand me a ring.

"You may kiss the bride," a distant voice said.

Sabine leaped straight up into my arms and kissed me. I held her close, clean off the ground with her legs hanging in midair. I didn't want to put her down. I didn't want to let her go. Of all the times we had hugged and kissed and held each other in those five years, none had come close to how I was feeling at that moment.

Later that night, I was sitting alone at the head table. We had had our dance and danced with our parents. We had eaten our dinner and cut the cake. She had thrown the flowers (not entirely by accident) into the arms of Keenan's date. So, I sat and watched the people we loved most in the world taking pictures together, drinking, and celebrating.

Keenan clapped me on the shoulder. "Hell of a party."

"Thanks. Looks like yours is next."

He gave a little intoxicated giggle. "Nah. Courthouse for me. Mom couldn't handle another wedding. Did you hear her today?" He suddenly became very sober. "I never have taken life too seriously. You really are a lucky guy and I hope I have even a fraction of your happiness."

"Thanks, man." I put my hand on top of his.

He wandered off towards his girlfriend. I spent so much of my life just being 'Keenan's brother' that I had never really thought that he really wanted for anything, least of all anything I had in my life.

I looked out into the crowd and found my wife, who had had far too much champagne, drunkenly shaking her hips on the dance floor with her matron of honor. My wife. I was completely flummoxed as to how such an amazing woman had chosen to spend the rest of her life with an average Joe like me. But we had just spoken the words.

To love and to cherish, in sickness and in health. We had both said those words and I had truly meant them. But did she? Here she sits in front of me, telling me she wants to end it all with no regard to how I feel.

Two years ago, she started to feel sick. We were terrified that she was pregnant; we already had a diabetic cat. But every test came back negative. I finally convinced her to go to the doctor. They sampled every body fluid they could collect from her. Two days later, her doctor made her drop everything and go to the university for emergency scans. She was irradiated, magnetized, and they used an ultrasound to collect samples with a needle that looked like it could impale her. I held her hand as long as they would let me be in the same room with her.

The next day they said what in the back of our minds we already knew. Cancer. She had a grapefruit-sized something in her abdomen and it looked aggressive. They wanted to shrink it before they tried to remove it. The combination of chemotherapy and radiation during that first three-month series almost killed her. She was strong at first but with each treatment, the vomiting worsened. She already had little weight to lose but she became frail and I could pick her up easily with one arm like a child. I tried to remain optimistic. I tried not to let her see how broken I felt. I wanted to make her better and watch her enjoy her favorite foods again. But I couldn't fix this.

When she had the mass removed, my mom, her parents, and Keenan all sat at the hospital in virtual silence for what felt like the entire day. The longer it took, the more hollow I felt. I couldn't eat but my mom got me to sip a sports drink. At long last they told us that she was in recovery. They had taken her spleen and part of her liver but they were not optimistic. She had a very long road ahead of her. I could not be strong anymore. I crumpled and cried. Keenan held me tightly as I sobbed. Months of pent-up sadness and pain poured out of me.

For more than a year she fought her body. Our lives became labyrinthine appointments and schedules. She worked until she couldn't anymore. Her parents helped her to doctor visits, blood sampling, and treatments while I had to work. In the evenings, she would lay in my arms as long as she could but every night, I saw a little more of the light in her eyes had faded. After her last scan, they finally told her there was little else they could do. It was aggressive and not responding to anything they tried. They could keep doing periodic chemo to keep it from growing as fast and try to manage the pain, but they couldn't stop it. There were experimental treatments that were showing promise at a facility several states away but we would have to move and experimental meant expensive. She said no.

She said no to all of it. She was done fighting. So here she sits in front of me. She is telling me it's over and that she's done.

"What about the life we were supposed to have together?" I ask, kneeling in front of her chair.

"We are thirty. You have plenty of life to look forward to. But I'd rather my life end while there's still some of me left. I don't want to rot away in a bed while you stand at my side, waiting for me to die."

I look at her hairless head and lashless eyes. I nod. I know she wants the pain to end, but what about my pain? I don't want to be shellfish but I can't help it.

"'Til death do us part." It is all I can think of to say.

"'Til death do us part." She takes my hands in hers and I lean my head towards her.

"I love you," she whispers.

I start to cry. "I love you." I gasp before the next sob.

I stay that way, weeping into her leg as she strokes my hair. I pull myself together enough to look up at the bag of fluids that has been keeping her alive since she hasn't been able to consistently digest anything. I move to look her in the eye and see a peace that wasn't there before. This is what she wants, what she needs, and I had promised to take care of her. We kiss as deeply as we dare in her condition as I slide ten little syringes full of insulin into her hand.

"Go," she whispers.

I see her look at the port in the IV line from the corner of my eye as I retreat. I close the door behind me. I stand, leaning against it for a few moments before I hear a little vocal sound escape her followed by sounds of her feet kicking against the floor and the chair groaning and creaking. I know it doesn't last long but it feels like she is seizing forever. Then, all is silent. I breathe again.

Goodbye Sabine.

25

H.

A poem in dedication to those who suffer.
One little girl
Holding hands in prayer
While teenage boy
Holds a gun on dare.
Mommy does weep
And hold teddy tight
While poor Daddy
Stays awake all night.
Auntie just drinks
While Uncle's away.
Granny one is sad
Grandad cried today.
Heaven I sit
And I watch them all.
I broke their hearts

When I chose to fall.
I did the things
I thought right for me.
I closed my eyes
To my family.
Just one more hit
And just one more drink.
One more. One more.
Did not stop or think.
Now I have died.
I have hurt them all.
No going back.
No chances at all.

26

Today

I am hollow today
An eggshell
Drained of yolk
If you drop me
I will break
I am empty today
A dried up well
A pit with no water
No life to give
Nothing to share
I am vast today
A void of darkness
No light inside
No sound within
Black and cold
I am dead today

My heart beats
My lungs breath
No emotion
Bleak and wasted

27

The Heating

The heat is intense today and the wind is carrying it in waves that roll like the tide. The parched ground releases little clouds of dust and remnants of long dehydrated vegetation. I sit in the sparse shade provided by our house while I strip a groundhog into usable meat, bones, and pelt. We had speared the little thing when we caught it trying to eat our vegetables. I know he was only trying to survive, but so are we. I look out over the field and watch my beloved toiling, trying to grow enough for us to eat through the winter. For as hot and dry as the summers have become, winters are frozen and desolate. If the heat of the sun in August does not kill you, being caught outside in January certainly will.

Life wasn't always this hard. Our ancestors enjoyed temperate climates and an abundance of food. My Nona said that once, there was so much food, people traded it all over the world. Now, you may trade with your neighbors but only if they have enough to spare and you have something of value.

My Nona's Nona told her they knew the earth was heating and food was getting harder to grow but they didn't want to believe it, so they chose not to. They continued to strip the ground of nutrients and pollute the sky. Drinkable water was used to keep grass green instead of people watered. Their lives were easy and it wasn't their problem. They had no concern for future generations.

As the planet became more strained, so did the people. Famine rode across the lands in a golden chariot with pestilence on a white horse following close behind. Wars became more frequent and intense as desperation for food and drinkable water consumed men. Bombs spewed more poison into the air and laid waste to more ground and in the end, only succeeded in making fewer humans who needed the resources. Of the nearly nine billion people at the beginning of the heating, only three billion survived.

So now, we do what we can with what is left. My beloved and I share a one-room home in the north, as far from the lethal heat of the equator as we could find shelter. I am glad for the groundhog meat. There are so few animals that survived the heating. Meat is a rare treat as most of our protein comes from the locusts and cicadas that thrive in the summer sun. Our ancestors had cows and chickens and other livestock to eat but large animals are too difficult to raise when water is rare and poultry is simply stolen. So, we tend the land, gather, and hunt just as the ancestors of our ancestors had done.

I lay the pelt of the groundhog on the ground next to me and look back out over the field. I see two men confronting my beloved and one is holding a rifle aimed at his chest. Ammunition is rare as the military hoards it all but there is a chance there may be a bullet in it. I lift my spear, still tipped with groundhog blood. I take aim and throw. I had never been a good distance marksman but my aim is true. The tip comes down in an ark, enters the juncture of the gunman's neck and shoulder, and lodges itself before exiting the ribcage. He tries to scream, likely more in surprise than in pain, but he cannot produce sound. He collapses, writhes a little, and stops moving. His companion looks at me in shock. I hold the knife I had been using to butcher the rodent and present it as if I mean to throw it at him. Rather than call my bluff, he looks down at his impaled friend… and flees.

I join my beloved in the field and we watch the man run. He picks up the rifle and checks it. There was indeed a single bullet. That will be traded in the spring for seeds and hard rations to come by such as flour, sugar, vinegar, and oil. I look back down at the man I have killed. At least now we will have meat through the winter.

28

My Own Story

"I had a dream about you," he said.

I froze. I knew that voice. It was a ghost from fourteen years ago. A voice I thought I would never hear again. Internally, I told myself to be brave. I steeled my nerves as I looked from the spot I had been mopping on the bookshop floor to the doorway.

He looked the same. Perhaps there were a few gray hairs and he was a little more round in the middle, but that face had hardly changed. His eyes, still young and blue as a sunny sky, looked straight into my heart. That heart quickened and I felt a little faint at the realization that he was really there. It had been fourteen years since we had said our final goodbye and he still had some kind of power over me.

"What are you doing here?" I leaned against the mop handle in part to hold myself up but also to appear more nonchalant than I felt.

"I had a dream that Melissa invited you to dinner. It was so real. I had to see you." He stepped into the shop and let the door close behind him. "You look exactly how I imagined. Still beautiful."

My heart did a strange flutter and my chest felt tight.

"What are you doing here?" I repeated.

He bit his lower lip and took a deep breath in through his nose before answering through his exhale. "Melissa's pregnant."

I stared at him. "And?"

"Did you hear me?" He stepped toward me. I moved the mop handle so it was between us as if it would shield me. He stopped. "I'm, going to be a dad."

"Congratulations." I was gripping the wooden handle so tightly my hands hurt.

I could see his jaw grinding before he spoke. "That's all you have to say?"

"What did you expect me to say?" I drew upon the little bit of courage I could muster. "I haven't seen you in a decade and a half. You've flown from the other side of the country to tell me your wife is pregnant." My voice shook a little less with each word as I spoke. "Why are you here?" I asked d a third time.

"Melissa's not my wife," he said coldly.

"How long have you lived together?" I asked.

"Seven years."

"She's your wife," I matched the ice in his voice.

"I love Melissa." He swallowed a lump in his throat. "But I'm in love with you."

I stared at him, stunned.

"Don't you miss me at all?" He asked.

Still staring at him in total disbelief, I felt my head shaking a slow but decisive no. "Miss you?" I squeaked.

"Don't you remember what we had?" He stepped toward me again.

I brandished the mop handle in front of me.

"Yes," I said clearly. The anxiety of being in his presence suddenly lifted. "I do remember. And I remember the eight years of therapy it took to undo enough of what you had done for me to feel like a human being again. I still have regular visits to help with the PTSD."

"PTSD!" He scoffed. "From what?"

"Do you remember my snow globe collection? Or how about my great-grandmother's measuring cups that just magically leaped off the hooks on the wall when you were mad at me?"

"Those were accidents," he reaffirmed.

"Was it an accident when I missed my family reunion because you didn't fix my car like you had promised? Or how about when I lost all of my friends because when I would come home you would berate me? You said me spending time with my friends and family made you feel like you weren't good enough for me."

"Well—"

"You said that I could talk to you so when I went out, I must be talking *about* you."

"Hang on—"

"You isolated me! You made everything my fault?"

"What was your fault?"

"It was my fault we didn't have money. It was my fault my

friends stopped talking to me. It was my fault when you broke my things. It was my fault when the house would be untidy.

My fault! My fault! My fault!" I was yelling now and suppressing my tears; I would not let him have the satisfaction of seeing me cry again.

"I did not isolate you. I always invited you out with my friends. And the house did get messy when you didn't clean. You knew I was too tired after work."

"*Your* friends were not *my* friends. Friends that I'd had since I was a teenager and lost. And what about the weekends? What about putting dishes in the dishwasher instead of the sink? Mowing the lawn took thirty minutes. For fuck's sake I broke my arm because you left laundry on the floor and I tripped over it and you blamed me for that too! I worked two jobs! I was tired too!"

He rolled his eyes. "We went over all of this when we were together."

"And it never changed! And that's why we aren't together anymore and haven't spoken in fourteen years."

"Us ending was a mistake," he said soothingly.

His tone, his inflection, and even the expression in his eyes triggered something deep inside me, something visceral. It was all familiar. This was the man who would explain why I was being stupid and irrational when we argued. That soothing voice would call me silly and tell me to calm down. If I dared stand up for myself, the voice would change to a roar and the soft eyes and passive expression would contort into something ugly and unholy.

"No. It wasn't." I looked him straight in the eye and spoke with clear definition.

His face flickered like the image on an old TV set but he regained composure in the bat of an eye.

"You stood by when your father told me to flush my dreams down the toilet because I was going to fail. You said nothing when your friend called me a drain and a waste," I continued.

"Honey, *if* that happened, they were drunk."

I scoffed. He knew they were drunk as if that were any excuse for him to not stand up for me.

"And you know I don't remember that actually happening. Your imagination has you angry for no reason," he nodded as if that would end the argument.

"Yeah. I know you claim you don't remember. So, either you're trying to gaslight me or you really have put it out of your mind. I'm betting it's the latter because you proved time and time again that things that were important to me – things that hurt me – weren't important to you."

His face flickered again and this time it seemed to take more effort to put it back together. You're just focusing on all of the bad things."

I pushed my lips together as hard as I could. I couldn't let the words in my brain fly out of my mouth. I would not let him goad me into a screaming match. Not again.

"You know why I focus on the bad things?" I narrowed my eyes at him. "Because there was so much more bad than good."

His visage was slipping again but he wasn't bothering to put the mask back on. "What about everything I did for you?"

A laugh that was more like a bark escaped me and I saw his eyes darken. "You know," I said. "That was the first thing you said to me when I told you I couldn't do this anymore. 'After everything I've done for you.' Those were your exact words. Because our relationship wasn't about love. You were no more in love with me then than you are pretending to be now. Our relationship was a transaction. Every dinner, every trip to the store, every time you fixed my car was an investment. You were purchasing my loyalty and the right to control me."

His face, I was sure, would be unrecognizable to almost anyone but me. His brows were pulled low over eyes that were no longer bright blue, but a cold, slate color. His jaw was locked and malice oozed from his skin.

"And you were innocent? You didn't use me for anything?" he growled.

"I was far from innocent. But I admitted to everything I had done. I admitted to taking more work to avoid coming home. I admitted I stopped talking to you in the end because I just wanted to lock you out and for it all to be over. I admitted I dragged out our misery because I didn't have the courage to cut you off like the diseased limb you were. And I apologized for all of it."

"So, you were emotionally abusive."

"Yes. But if I made you so miserable, why didn't you leave? If I was so abusive, why were you angry when I ended it instead of being relieved?" He opened his mouth but I cut him off. "Because I was relieved. I was scared of surviving on my own, but I was relieved. And I have never regretted it."

The set in his jaw shifted. "Yes, you do."

"No." I shook my head again. "You need to go back to Texas and back to Melissa and your baby and never think of me again for the rest of your life because I won't be thinking of you. And should we see each other when we're both dead and in Hell, don't speak to me then either."

He chewed on his tongue and finally broke eye contact. "Melissa left me."

I hadn't expected that confession but I was far from surprised. "Why?"

"She said ours wasn't the kind of relationship she wanted to raise a child in. I came home from work and she was gone. That was three months ago."

I nodded solemnly. I finally understood. "So, you lost control of your wife and thought you could come back and try to regain control of me."

"No." He was a good liar, but not this time.

"She's smart. She's putting that baby first. It's unfortunate that it took her seven years and a pregnancy but then again it took me nine." He charged for me and I once again brandished the mop I'd forgotten I was holding. "You know, you called me selfish and manipulative. But it's not selfish for Melissa and me to want lives that we aren't afraid of or manipulative for us to escape."

His jaw moved as he ground his molars. "You need me."

"I haven't for more than fourteen years. I think I'll be all right."

He glared but didn't say anything else. He spun, hit the door HARD with his open palm, and marched into the parking lot. I heard tires squeal and saw a black sedan – probably a rental – speed out onto the street.

All of the strength that had held me together for that entire encounter suddenly fled my body. I finally released my grip on the mop handle and it crashed to the floor with me close behind. On my knees, I wrapped my arms around myself and pressed my forehead to the floor. I intermittently held my breath and gasped for air, trying to find myself. He had really been here. In *my* store. I had actually *spoken to him*. For years after we had ended, I had known that if he ever reappeared in my life, I would not be strong enough to resist him. I would have gladly wrapped myself in the cocoon of familiarity. At the time, it seemed preferable to struggling to make it on my own, fighting to find my identity, and discovering my voice. But I had done it. Not only that, but I had just used that voice to say all of the things that needed to be said and to tell him never to come back.

I lifted my head and looked at the books on the shelves of my shop. In their pages were the likes of Joan of Arc, Medea, Hester Prynne, and other amazing women who fought demons and dragons and men. I felt like one of them. I had fought my demon and become the heroine of my own story.

29

Written in the Hotel in Chicago

A drop of rain
upon my head
on the day
I am to wed.
My love does smile.
My heart does sink.
My mind clouds.
It's hard to think.
A future bright.
The unknown grim.
Forever
I'm bound to him.
Drop. Drop. The rain
falls from the sky.

Heaven weeps.
I'll never fly.
Like a clipped bird
trapped on the ground.
In a cage.
Screams without sound.
He says "I do"
and I do too.
My fate is sealed.
My future true.

30

Love and Lust

The light I see
May not be
For me
And guides another man.
Tis shining bright
In the night
To fight
True love's forbidden hand.
Love may be lust.
Beauty must
Be thrust
In front of my blind eyes
May love be true,
Not undue
For you.
My heart is telling lies.

31

Flower Mirror

    Sweet scent.
Oh, nectar of life.
Beauty of all
Nature of light.

A leaf,
Envy shown in green.
Truth of all
Left to be seen.

Petals.
They reflect the heart.
Red love. Blue hate.
Reflections part.

Earth roots

Holding to the ground
Anchor the soul
And hold one down.

Sharp thorns
Hold villains at bay,
Protect the weak.
Live a new day.

32

Turkey Shoot

I used to have a temper. It was a pretty nasty one. My mother, devil rest her soul, attributed to my flaming red hair. This is nonsense, of course. If dinner was cold, it would be on the floor or the wall. If I would break the tip of my pencil, it would be stabbed through the notebook cover to cover. I earned a reputation for being "the biter" in preschool. I learned shortly after starting grade school that if I wanted friends, I would need to control myself. I learned to suppress my rage, to push it deep down inside of me and not let it escape. Time would eventually squelch the rage but until then, I would be outwardly normal. All I needed was time to swallow it and digest it.

November is always a difficult month for me. My father had died Thanksgiving night when I was only 19 years old. He meant the world to me. He took care of my mom and protected us from the world. But he also taught me the importance of being strong and being able to care for myself. Without a son to pass his masculine wisdom to, he placed it all squarely on my shoulders and I was glad to carry the burden. He instilled in me the importance of family and taking care of your own. He taught me how to manage finances, change my oil, and how to till a vegetable garden. Most importantly, he taught me how to hunt.

Every fall on a random day that he would deem as "perfect," he would wake me up before the sun and we would drive to some prechosen destination in the middle of nowhere. We would set up a base camp and wait. Sometimes we hunted turkey, sometimes rabbit, and occasionally deer. It all depended on what he was in the mood for. I didn't particularly like the killing part. We used every bit of the animals; we ate the meat, mom would make soup from the bones, and we would sell the pelts so I didn't feel as guilty. But Dad said I was a natural killer whether I liked it or not. He said it was part of my nature and I couldn't fight my nature. I doubted all that but he was right about one thing; I was good. I rarely missed whether it was with a shotgun or a bow.

Mostly, I just enjoyed the peace and solitude of being out there. There were no honking cars or screaming kids. It was a place for reflection. It was a place to find myself. My whole life I kept a bag and quick-tent packed and ready to run away at a moment's notice.

When Dad died, Mom and I had a bit of a falling out. He had been hit by a drunk driver but not killed instantly. I had been on the other side of the country at school when it happened. I had chosen not to come home for the holiday, much to their dismay. She was angry with me for not being with him when he passed. She didn't need to be angry with me. I was mad at myself. I was at a party and didn't get my mother's hundred messages until the next morning. I tried to get home to him, but I didn't make it in time. After the funeral, I returned to school and stayed far away from the West Coast where I wouldn't have to feel so much shame every time I looked at her.

While in school, I met Alex. He was everything I never knew I needed. We had met when I was twenty-one and he was twenty-three. He had approached me in the coffee shop on campus and asked if I knew how amazing my smile was. I still get butterflies thinking about that. He was warm and affectionate. He listened to my day at work and pampered me in a way I never knew possible. He was the only man to tell me I was beautiful. I truly counted myself lucky. We were together for five years before he asked me to be with him forever. We made it another two years but I never got to walk down the aisle.

November of 2019 was a month I will never forget. I thought I was working my dream job and was set to climb that ladder faster than any of my predecessors. I was sent to exchange vows with the man of my dreams in less than a month. Life was golden.

Tuesday:

I woke up for work early. I had my coffee and ate my power bar. I dressed and pressed. I kissed Alex's forehead before I headed off to work. I was on top of the world. I hardly noticed the moving van across the street when I left.

Work that day was hard. There were rumors abound that layoffs were coming. I didn't see how that could be possible.

The company was poised to report record profits that year. I tried to calm everyone and remind them all that hard work would keep them off the chopping block. I didn't want to believe it could be happening but when my supervisor- a no nonsense kind of man- was scared, it was hard not to be nervous.

When I came home, I stepped onto almost foreign soil. The carpet was mine. The dining table was mine. The couch, television, and even the pictures off the wall were all gone. On the kitchen counter were a key, the box for my ring, and a sticky note with 'I'm sorry. I can't' written on it.

I felt a great pressure well up in my ribs. It was pain. It was rage. The pressure strangled my chest and I tried desperately to force air into my lungs. I screamed with what breath I had to relieve it, but it wasn't enough. I crumpled to the floor in a ball and instead forced it all down inside as much as I could. I cried myself to sleep that night on the floor with a single pillow and quilt that he had left for me.

Wednesday:

I had failed to set my alarm that night so Wednesday morning, I awoke after 8am. I jumped out of the "bed" I had made on the floor. I threw on the first clothes I found, didn't bother with makeup, and pulled my hair into something that resembled a bun. Despite my rush, I was still more than two hours late to work. All through the day, I had trouble focusing. I couldn't compose a proper e-mail to save my life and I missed phone calls despite sitting next to it at my desk. At 4pm, I was pulled into my boss's office.

"I'm sorry," he said. "I know it's just one bad day but the men upstairs are not impressed with what they've seen today."

"What do you mean?" I asked, feeling the pressure I had not quite controlled beginning to boil up again.

"Well, they've been talking about rearranging some things here. Getting rid of some positions. They've been watching everyone closely all week and, well, you're the first one they've decided to let go."

"You... you can't mean it." The pressure was now pushing on my eyes and forcing out the tears.

"Please," he said as he looked at his hands. "Got clean out your desk and return your badge to security."

Thursday:

I didn't get out of bed. I didn't eat. I didn't even turn on the TV. I just stayed hidden under the quilt on the floor. In the evening, I got a phone call. It was from my mother. It was Thanksgiving Day. She always called on the anniversary of Dad's passing. I don't know why. Loneliness maybe? She was never kind when she called but every year, she seemed to get more and more bitter. This year was the worst. She made a pretense to be cordial. She asked how my life was going so far away from family. I told her about Alex leaving and losing my job. She started to laugh hysterically.

"What's so funny?" I asked.

"I'm sorry, but I knew Karma would come get you some day."

"Karma? What did I do to deserve this?"

"You abandoned your family. You ran away. You left your father to die in the hospital without saying goodbye!"

I hung up on her and buried my face deeper into my soggy pillow. I felt the pressure – the rage – returning. It was boiling inside me like water in a tea kettle. I threw my phone and it smashed against the wall.

Friday:

Something struck me early in the morning. I had to go away. I couldn't keep wallowing. I needed to get away and clear my head. I needed time for all of the hurt and anger to tame down. The woods. The woods were my sanctuary. There were no phones, no e-mails, no deadlines, no fiancées, no mothers...I would trek into the trees with my gear, find a good deer path, and leave the world behind.

I headed to my favorite quick-trip hideaway. My dad and I would vanish into that perfect Oregon wilderness for days at a time whenever the mood struck him. While the mountains in Kentucky offered a different kind of forest, it was still therapeutic. Two hours in the car was a small price to pay for two days in the middle of nowhere. I parked at my favorite trailhead, put my camping permit in the windshield, and started on the trail.

The area could get a little bit tourist-y if you didn't know where to go. I always listened to the locals. Deer can always lead you to great hideaways. I followed the human path until it intersected with a worn wildlife trail. Anyone who didn't know what they were looking for (or weren't looking at all) would have missed it.

I followed it along through the trees deeper and deeper into the unknown. The longer I hiked, the more I could feel the tension in my shoulders release. The puffiness in my face from days of crying seemed to dissipate. I breathed the rich, cold air and listened to the late birds singing above me. I could hear sticks snapped by unseen creatures here and there as they fled from me. All the while, I knew there was no one around, but I couldn't shake the feeling that I was being followed. It was fall, but it I kept on guard in case I was being hunted by a bear.

I walked along a ledge that followed a watershed until it opened up to a wide creek bed. This was it. I pitched my tent, gathered wood, and set up a fire ring. All the while, I couldn't shake that feeling that I was being watched. I kept my rifle in site. It took several hours, but my little oasis was open for business. By that point, it was long passed lunch and headed towards supper time. The sun was tucking behind the cliffs as I ate the can of soup I had heated over the fire. At one point, I swore I heard human coughing. I aimed my flashlight in all directions but saw nothing. I hadn't heard any footsteps approaching so I decided it was my imagination. With a hearty stew in my belly, I laid back and watched the stars wake up one by one. There were a few crickets and frogs refusing to hibernate that began their lullabies and sang me off to sleep.

In the morning, I stripped down and lowered myself into the creek. Nothing could wake you up faster than a cold creek bath. I lay back in the water and felt more like myself than I had all week.

I heard a branch break and a flash of orange tumbled down the side of the ridge and landed in my campsite. The hunter scrambled to his feet.

"I-I'm sorry." He stammered and averted his gaze.

I was on my feet. I looked him up and down. He was short and thin with a bushy brown mustache. He wore cheap camo under the orange vest and a turkey call protruded from his breast pocket.

Turkey season had ended weeks ago. He was a poacher. This little ferret of a man was disturbing my solitude. The stress that had dissipated the day before came back tenfold.

"How long were you up there?" I was standing in the water, fully unclothed, and I didn't care.

He looked at me and turned away again.

"You followed me here." I put my hands on my hips. Internally I was boiling over with rage. Externally, I tempered my tone and body language to mildly annoyed.

"I'm sorry," he said again.

I'm sorry. I had been told that all week. I'm sorry. Alex was sorry that after seven years of our lives together, he couldn't marry me. He was sorry for breaking my heart. My boss was sorry I had had a bad day. He was sorry he had to fire me. My mother *claimed* she was sorry that bad things were happening to me but I deserved it for not being by my father's side. Now this pervert was sorry he had followed me. He was sorry he had watched me bathe. No, he was sorry he was caught. Everyone was sorry but no one knew what *sorry* was.

I walked out of the water. "Sorry." I said as I picked up my rifle.

I saw the look in his eyes change from fear to terror. He ran. He took off down the creek bed as fast as he could. I watched him stumble over loose rocks and splash in shallow water in his haste.

I brought the site up to my eye. Dad always said I was a natural killer. And I don't miss. Before I realized what I was doing, I saw the orange go down into the water. Everything around me was silent. I saw the red trickle down with the water until it touched my toes. I had just killed a man in cold blood. I should have felt something but I saw all of them, all the people who had apologized to me, laying there in that creek and I realized that all of the pressure that had building was suddenly gone.

33

Shadow, shadow.

Shadow, shadow,
Dark as night.
Across the ground
You do take flight.
Carry secrets
Spare no souls
Whisper whispers
No one's told
Shadow, shadow,
Winged beast.
The lies you tell
Know no peace.
Hunger, Anger.
Empty words.
Death be suffered
Life not heard.

34

An Excerpt from Angel's Seed

"Sorry I'm late!" Danny made a beeline straight for the coffee pot. "I got a little tied up this morning."

I rolled my eyes. "Uh-huh. And what was this one's name?"

"Caroline." He paused with the coffee mug a few inches from his mouth. "I think." He took his cell phone from his back pocket and looked at it. "Oops. Rachel."

"One of these days you're going to get one of these women pregnant and you'll have to remember her name."

"Nah." He shook his head. "I've got deadbeat dad written all over me. Just need to know where to send the support check." He took a big swig of coffee. "You know, track star, a date here and there might be good for you."

"I do date," I replied indignantly.

"You hole up in your house night after night grading

papers and playing videogames. You have half a classroom full of beautiful girls whose grades could probably use a boost."

"That's unethical."

"Ethics are only suggestions." He smiled. "You taught me that."

"That's not at all what I meant. One day you'll have to grow up."

"Yeah, maybe. But today is no that day."

35

If I Died Tomorrow

If I died tomorrow
Will anyone see?
If I died tomorrow
Will anyone miss me?
If my lungs ceased to breathe
Will anybody mind?
Will they find my body
If my breath froze in time?
If my heart no longer beat
Will any people cry?
If my chest stopped moving
Will people bat an eye?
If The Powers end my life
And I do not resist
Will the world ever see?
Will I even be missed?

36

The Ornament

My favorite part of Christmas is going through the boxes of ornaments. It's like traveling through time and each figurine is a stop along the way.

Here is the little wooden horse my Papaw made me just before he died. He put so much time and effort into the intricate details. That man put true tenderness and love into everything he did; including taking care of me when I was little. He was the only one who nurtured my love of horses and riding. He always knew he could find me in the barn and he taught me how to ride just as well as any of the men, even though I was still a little girl. I couldn't have asked for a better person to look up to. I was truly devastated when he succumbed to cancer.

Here is the little ceramic ballet slipper from my aunt. She had insisted that I start dance classes when I was four years old. She believed I needed to grow up with grace and elegance. She kept a nagging voice in my ear all the way up until I was a teenager. I know she meant well, but after I left home at eighteen, I didn't miss it.

Here's the little globe my dad gave me. He told me that I could go anywhere in the world my heart dared take me. Like Papaw, he saw strength in me and encouraged it. The women in my family insisted that I be a lady. I had to dress right and act accordingly. I had to speak with perfect grammar and I must never use a contraction or words like "very." Not Daddy or Papaw. They told me I could be anything I wanted. When Daddy disappeared a few years after Papaw died, my heart was broken again. I was left with *them*. That's why when I turned eighteen, I left and never looked back.

My aunts and my mother meant well. I do believe that. But they made no effort to understand me at all. After I'd lost Papaw and Daddy, I felt utterly alone. My life was consumed by dresses and tea. I didn't relate to my cousins at all. Any time I was dirty or my hair wasn't right, I was chided. My cousins would hold their noses and ask who let in the cow when I would walk by.

School wasn't any better. I didn't fit in with the other girls who wanted designer clothes and handbags. I had virtually no friends outside of the barn. My debutante ball, while used as a charity benefit, was humiliating. I felt like a cupcake that my aunts were attempting to auction off to the highest bidder.

I got in my old, busted, Saturn SL2 and drove. I didn't care where I went, as long as it wasn't home. I slept in my car at truck stops and gas stations for days. Massachusetts was behind me and that was all that mattered. Maybe I'd go to California. May I could be a showgirl in Vegas until I could earn enough money to really travel. My mind reeled with possibilities. But, none of them came to fruition.

Shortly after I crossed into Colorado from Nebraska, my poor little car gave out. I hitched a ride (yes, I know how dangerous that is) into a little town in Logan County called Padroni. This tiny nook in the world was called home by a whopping eighty residents. It became eighty-one.

I couldn't help but awe at the town's charm. It was a simple slice of suburbia surrounded by nothingness. It was quiet, quaint, and nothing like New England. Outside of town, on Route 48, the Neely family had a small ranch and hired me to tend the horses. They set up an outbuilding as a small apartment for me and I lived and worked there. It was a perfect corner of heaven.

After a few months of working, I had saved up enough money to return home (by plane) and collect my things. My aunt and mother protested and argued but there was nothing they could do. I had finally found somewhere I felt like I belonged.

For my first Christmas in my new home, I went into nearby Sterling to buy a little tree. As I meandered down Main Street, braced against the cold a very handsome man caught my eye. Even through his coat, I could tell he was well-muscled. He was tall with dark hair and dark eyes. His skin was naturally tanned which helped him stand out more in the crowd. He smiled at me and nodded his head. I returned the gesture and I'm sure I blushed a little. My mother and aunt were so bent on match-making me with a 'good' family that I hadn't really dated much in high school. I bought my tree and took it home in the bed of the red Chevy truck I'd traded my

Saturn for. It barely ran, but at least it was mine and practical given my new habitat.

On Christmas Eve, the youngest Neely, Matthew, came and knocked on my door. He was only seven years old. A cute kid.

I opened the door. "Hello, Mattie. What can I do for you?"

He smiled wide. "Will you come have hot chocolate with us?"

The Neely's had invited me to join them for dinner several times but I always felt awkward. They were my employers and while I didn't have any family or friends out here, it felt strange to accept any more of the hospitality and warmth they had already given me. But, this time... It was Christmas. I slid into my boots and jacket, took little Mattie's hand, and let him escort me across the field to the big house.

Charlotte, the matriarch of the family, welcomed me with open arms. "I'm so glad you came! No one should be alone for Christmas! Let me take your coat."

Mattie took my hand once again and escorted me into the living room. There was Dan, the father, Kimmy, the nine-year-old daughter, and a few other faces I didn't recognize. Then my eyes fell on someone who seemed familiar.

Charlotte bustled in behind me. "This is my sister, Tammy, her husband, John, and their kids Mikey and Amanda. Over there is Dan's brother, Greg, and his wife, Patricia." Then she gestured at the handsome man I had seen in Sterling. "And this is Dan's nephew, Jason."

He reached out and shook my hand. It felt so small and cold enclosed in his but I felt a rush of heat to my face. The evening was perfect. We sat and sipped cocoa and listened to

Christmas music. They all had a million questions about me but I was really only interested in one of them.

Jason had just come home from the military. He was originally from Boulder but was staying with his uncle until he decided what he really wanted to do with his life. He'd planned on college but wasn't sure for what. He said he was twenty-two and had plenty of time to figure things out. I was completely enthralled by him.

As the evening drew to a close, Kimmy came up and set a box in my hand. "We wanted to give you this in case Santa had trouble finding you this year. You can't open it 'til tomorrow though."

I was touched. I almost cried. I hadn't been expecting any Christmas presents at all. I looked up at Charlotte and Dan. They smiled back at me.

I looked down at Kimmy. "Thank you, so much!" I hugged the little girl.

"Why don't I walk you back?" Jason was putting on his coat.

I smiled at him. "That would be lovely."

I said my goodbyes and received hugs – I never got hugs from my own family – and Jason took my arm and escorted me back to my little cabin.

We stood at the door. "You, Miss Miranda, are a very interesting person."

I blushed again. I really wished I could stop doing that. "I am?"

"Yes. And I'd like to take you to dinner sometime away from the family to learn more about you if that'd be alright." His slightly western drawl (compared to my very New England dialect) was honey to my ears.

"I believe I would enjoy that, Mr. Neely."

"No, Ma'am. Just Jason."

I smiled. "Okay, Just Jason. I look forward to hearing from you."

He smiled too. He kissed my hand and headed back to the house. This was the kind of thing every little girl dreamt of. I went into my cabin and placed my present under my tiny tree. I was so excited to have something to open in the morning.

Christmas day came. I woke, made my coffee, and sat on the floor in front of the tree. My mother had never been a fan of the "raucous chaos" most children made when tearing into presents so I had been conditioned to wait my turn. What was I doing? It was just me. I tore through the wrapping paper and threw the pieces into the air just for the Hell of it. I giggled. I could hear my mother gasping in dismay. I opened the little box and inside was a glass icicle ornament. It was beautiful. I hung it on my tree carefully and sat back admiring it while I finished my coffee.

I dressed and called home. I was two hours behind my mother so I was sure she would be out of church. She was probably at my aunt's house overseeing the cooking of the evening feast. I was going to miss out on apple pumpkin soup, beef rib roast, mashed potatoes, and maple carrots. It was okay though. I had bought my own vegetables and a little beef roast for myself. It wasn't quite going to be a feast, but it would do.

I put my boots on and readied to go check on the horses. I opened the door and screamed. Jason stood with his fist ready to knock and scared the daylights out of me.

"I'm so sorry. I was coming to see if I could walk out to the barn with you. The kids are going crazy in there."

I laughed. "That's quite alright. I would love some company."

He smiled. He helped me check hooves, freshen water, and pitch hay chips. I brought out a bag of apples I had been saving for them for a special treat.

"Did ya like your ornament?" He patted one of the barn cats tenderly.

"Yes. Very much."

"Good. The kids heard we get less snow here than you do back home and they were afraid you'd miss it. That's why they picked an icicle."

"That was very sweet of them."

"What are you doing for Christmas dinner?"

"I have a roast and I'm going to try my hand at maple carrots and onion mashed potatoes."

"Maple carrots? Like maple syrup? And beef?"

"Yes. Is that not what is traditional here?"

"No. We eat ham. And corn and beans. And lots of bread."

"I think that sounds as strange to me as maple carrots do to you." I laughed. "I think you're right. Does sound good though. There's enough for two if you would like to join me." I couldn't believe I'd had the courage to ask.

"You know what? I think I'd like to take you up on that. I'm sure Aunt Char wouldn't mind."

My heart leaped. I was having a real Christmas after all.

When we got back to my cabin, I cleaned vigorously. My mother had always taught me that a dirty house meant a dirty host and I couldn't allow that. Thankfully it was really only one room (save for the bathroom). I didn't have the cloth napkins or elaborate centerpiece that I was accustomed to, but I made do the best I could.

Dinner was perfect. It tasted awful. I hadn't grown up in the kitchen. But the company and the atmosphere were more than I could have ever hoped for. He had brought a bottle of wine and we got a little giggly after dinner. He spent the night that night. I will save you the details there; a lady doesn't kiss and tell.

We were head-over-heels. Instead of going to college, he stayed to work on the ranch. He tended the cows and chickens while I cared for the horses. After two years, he moved into the little cabin on the Neely property with me. Life was perfect. Almost.

I started to notice a change in him. He no longer kissed me before we went our separate ways to care for the ranch. He stopped making excuses to join me when I went into town and would not tell me where he was going when he left without me. Some nights I sat up drinking wine alone. When I confronted him, we would often end up yelling. In a home with no walls, there was nowhere to hide and he would often leave and go stay at the big house or disappear for the night. I felt more secluded than I ever had since moving to Colorado.

On our fifth Christmas, I was in Sterling to look for gifts for my adopted family. I rounded a store corner and saw Jason kissing another woman. My heart was ripped from my chest. I felt sick. I fled back to my truck and home. Why? How long had this been going on?

When he came home, I confronted him. He said her name was Anne. He knew her from his life in Boulder and she had moved to Sterling more than a year ago. They had picked up where they had left off but he didn't have the heart to tell me.

I'm not sure what happened. I remember thinking that I couldn't let him leave me like every other man I'd loved. Papaw had withered away. Daddy just disappeared one day. I couldn't lose Jason too. I just couldn't. The next thing I knew, I was standing over him with the glass ice icicle in my hand, covered in blood. The sun was receding further behind the hills as I felt the shaking subside. I released my grip on the ornament. I could see the impression from the glass and my own fingernails from gripping it so tightly in the palm of my hand.

I calmly placed it in a bowl of peroxide. While it soaked, I looked down at his bloody body. He had been so handsome and kind. Why did he do this to me? I retrieved some plastic sheeting from the barn and wrapped him carefully in it, securing the bundle with duct tape. I pulled up the floorboards and rolled him into the crawlspace below. He wasn't going to leave me. Not now.

I told the family we had gotten into a fight and he had left. The police were called. There were search parties in the hills; since his truck was still at our house, he couldn't be far. They believed me, not knowing how close to home he really was, but never finding him.

That was two years ago. Here's the little rocking horse ornament Kimmy had made me the year Jason disappeared. Here's the silver horseshoe I had bought for myself my second year here. Here are the two turtle doves we got the year we announced our engagement. And here is the icicle that kept him from leaving me.

37

New Year

New year.
New me.
Freedom as
it ought to be.
No more work.
No longer slave.
Striking out.
I must be brave.
Freedom comes
at heavy cost.
I must remember
what I've lost.
My heart does ache.
This is true.
I thought I would
be lost without you.

But this I must.
Forced to endure.
The love I felt
is no longer pure.
Your lies and screams
Cut like a Knife.
This is not what
I want for life.
This new year
will be mine.
The wounds will heal.
It will take time.
New year.
New me.
Peace at Last.
As it should be.

www.ingramcontent.com/pod-product-compliance
Lightning Source LLC
LaVergne TN
LVHW021806060526
838201LV00058B/3257